WOOD
FOR WOOD-CARVERS
AND CRAFTSMEN

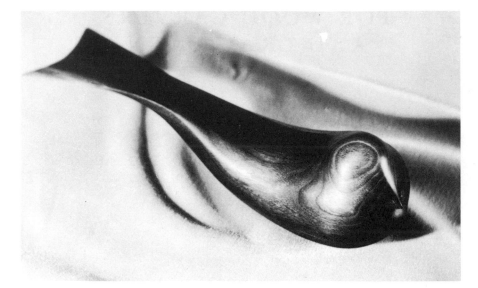

How long did the nut tree grow
Where barked the fox, and rains
Fell light on leaf, and moon glow
Found the sleeping bird on its bough?
What years fell when came the cut,
Sweet smelling chips of time
Arched out by the axe? But
The final marvel! The dreaming eye
Looking far beneath the bark to see
Deep in the webbed wood where waiting
For the—skilled hand to free
Sat this velvet-brown, demure dove
                    Mary Hoffman Schuldenfrei

WOOD
FOR WOOD-CARVERS
AND CRAFTSMEN

Source, Selection, Cutting, Treatment, Drying of Flitches, and Guidance in Their Use

Robert L. Butler

South Brunswick and New York: A. S. Barnes and Company
London: Thomas Yoseloff Ltd

© 1974 by A. S. Barnes and Co., Inc.

A. S. Barnes and Co., Inc.
Cranbury, New Jersey 08512

Thomas Yoseloff Ltd
Magdalen House
136-148 Tooley Street
London SE1 2TT, England

Library of Congress Cataloging in Publication Data

Butler, Robert L
  Wood for wood-carvers and craftsmen.

  Bibliography: p.
1. Wood. 2. Wood-carving. I. Title.
TT186.B87   745.51   73-10513
ISBN 0-498-01376-6

to
FAYE
who knows the
Wood Carvers'-Craftsmen Syndrome

Contents

Acknowledgments

I was fortunate to have a fine friend in Dr. Wayne Murphey, professor of Wood Technology, at Pennsylvania State University. He took time out from a busy schedule of research and teaching to review critically the first and second draft. His valuable suggestions for additions and his help in rationalizing some of my observation with the correct reasoning helped me in following the admonition of Epictetus. I was particularly delighted that he permitted my writing alternative explanations that were within truth but not of common usage in the profession of wood technology.

Linda Nihart typed without complaint the many revisions of sections and the final manuscript. She saved me much time in the preparation of figures 35 through 38 and figure 47.

Rae Chambers, fellow biologist and illustrator, prepared to my great satisfaction figures 10 and 41 on tree growth, wood structure and shrinkage.

Susan C. Ferris of A. S. Barnes and Company, Inc., broke all records in returning my manuscript with editorial corrections and changes. What a delight!

I was greatly pleased that The American Forestry Association through Richard Pardo, administrative assistant, permitted me to use the AFA's *Social Register of Big Trees*. Readers should note that the register is updated frequently in *American Forests*, magazine of the American Forestry Association.

Michael C. Contezac, information specialist, of the Forest Products Laboratory at Madison, Wisconsin graciously granted the use of material in figure 40 and table 8.

Permission to photograph the carvings of Nelson Wood of Boalsburg, Pennsylvania, and Maurice Ganter of Mechanicsville, Pennsylvania, was given with great kindness and patience.

Cecil Carstenson, well-known author and wood sculptor of

Kansas City, Missouri, was very gracious to take time from his work to review the first draft manuscript and offer much encouragement.

George Nakashima, artist-craftsman of New Hope, Pennsylvania, approved my using two of his beautiful expressions on the subject of wood.

Introduction

A new era is dawning; modern man is demanding and exploring ways in which he can express his latent creativity. He longs to use his hands in ways other than pushing pencils, solving equations, writing orders, repairing cars, or fixing water faucets. He has accepted the plastics and metals of modern technology, but finds these cold and aesthetically undesirable. There exists a desire to create something out of the roughest beginnings in nature.

Wood has long served man in the construction of home and in the fashioning of primitive and simple tools for use in home, field and forest. It served as material for the expression of his early art. Man's early organic relationships are being renewed.

Individuals who had never known the joy of creativity have turned to crafting fine furniture and to wood carving as a serious hobby. The vice-president of the National Wood Carvers Association, Donald Fenner, in the January-February, 1972, issue of *Chip Chats* has described the problems of the association as it approaches a membership of 10,000. In 1968 there were only 1,500 members. Special workshops and centers now offer from two to ten weeks of special training in wood carving. Wood carving and furniture construction are being taught throughout the nation in adult education courses. Regional art festivals feature wood sculptors and craftsmen. Man is rediscovering himself and the potential for his creativity in wood.

The author views wood carving as the art form involving all the senses. In common with all other art, vision plays the largest part. Carving in the round demands approval of an infinity of views. The painter, to the contrary, is constrained to use two dimensions in attempting three.

Touch, the second most important sense, plays a prominent part. The sculptor is compelled to move his hands over the form he is fashioning after each sequence of cuts. For a blind person this is thigmotactic, three-dimensional sight. Sculpture through touch communicates form and texture.

All wood-carvers and craftsmen know that each wood has its own unique odor, sometimes a delightful fragrance, sometimes a questionable aroma. Admittedly, the painter may enjoy the fragrance of turpentine and oils, but the wood-carver is exposed to an array of odors limited only by the variety of woods he uses.

Taste, one of the two most subtle senses of the wood-carver, is experienced during the final moments of sanding and finishing. The dust he invariably inhales reaches his palate. He learns that each wood has its own taste and therefore is tempted to taste the product of his labors. In any event, I often chew the wood chips of my work.

Several years ago I had the good fortune to hear Carleen Hutchins present a seminar on the family of violins in the Physics Department at Penn State University. For the past 22 years she has been deeply involved as a member of the Cat Gut Ascoustical Society in exploring the "secrets" of great string instruments (Hutchins, 1962 and 1967). On the day of her seminar she demonstrated the tonal qualities and especially the timbre (not timber) of different woods. "Fiddleback" maple and rosewood were remarkably brilliant as resonators. Basswood and pine were poor in comparison. I note that the wood-carver, Cecil C. Carstenson (1971), obtained some or his Brazilian rosewood from a pile of rejected marimba bars. Although it is coincidental that he refers to the subject of my first chapter in the same words, "Wood is where you find it," he made no reference in the course of his excellent book to the timbre of wood. He did, however, refer to the poor resonance of blocks of wood having internal rot, hidden rocks or internal spaces caused by improper drying. All woods can be distinguished as having different quality as resonators.

The stimuli provided to our sense of vision, touch, smell, taste, and hearing communicates more ideas and feelings than can be found in other forms of art. These form a gradient of intensity diagramed as follows:

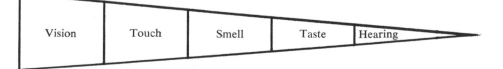

Development and growth of these capacities to experience wood recalls to man a wholesome and primitive bond with his organic past.

Unfortunately the creativity of the wood-carver or craftsman too often begins with an unspecified block or slab of wood, one that he has purchased, but not selected, from a supply house. Not many can visit his supplier and personally choose a piece. He is restricted to those species offered and further restricted by the available shapes and sizes. Adjustment of his thinking to such a piece of wood is a constraint to creativity.

The purpose of this book is to remove the constraint of a limited wood supply and thereby provide a new potential for creativity. In the shop, basement, or garage should be a variety of species in all manner of shapes and sizes that constantly pique the curiosity of the wood-carver, sculptor, and craftsman.

The author will share his experience in exploring sources of wood and the selection and precise method of cutting flitches suitable for carving or further cutting. Emphasis will be given to the special treatment and storage, with details on the techniques of drying small to large flitches. A new experience is at hand: sculpting from tree to final form or crafting from tree to furniture coupled with an escape from lumberyards and high-priced specialty shops of exotic and domestic wood.

Those exposed to wood through sculpturing or in creating fine furniture develop a love for wood that verges on obsession. The syndrome is characterized as a desire to learn the features of all species of trees, to sculpt, craft, and collect supplies, and to experience each species through all the senses.

The reader who takes this book seriously will not escape wood-carver's syndrome. Ask any wood-carver's family about one of the most time-consuming symptoms of this affliction. It is not the cost of tools that threatens family ties, but the expenditure of time and energy in sighting and acquiring wood. Enroute to family picnics and vacations the non-wood-carvers in the car soon learn to hate the sight of a jumble of logs. The lives of the riders are in jeopardy, for the driver gives more vision to wood than to road. Each magnificent potential at road, dam, new building site, or orchard undergoing renovation must be investigated—no matter how long it takes to contact the farmer or the construction boss. The following weekend is lost for the family in a return to the area with chain saw, peavey, and trailer to cut and choose those treasures rescued

FIGURE 1. The author's lode of flitches, representing many domestic species in a great variety of shapes and sizes.

from the fire or dump. Soon every corner of basement, garage (figure 1), and house is filled with blocks of wood stacked to the rafters in different stages of drying. Hopefully, the family understands this malady and is willing to wait for the products of the studio and shop—to say nothing of the income. He is permitted his indulgence. The affliction does not abate, but continues to deepen with keeness of vision in recognizing species and judgment as to quality of the lode seen.

WOOD
FOR WOOD-CARVERS
AND CRAFTSMEN

1

Wood Is Where You Find It

Many books are available on wood-carving, giving information on the tools to use, how to use them, how to sharpen them, and the quality and specifications of various species of wood. Ah, but there is the rub. Where does one get the wood for wood carving and the crafting of unique furniture? Wood is where you find it. Strange as it may seem, it is most unlikely to be purchased at the local lumberyard.

The experienced wood-carver learned in his earlier years the disappointment that wood for wood-carvers cannot be purchased at what seemed the most likely source. The lumberyard plays to the gallery of construction, not the artist's studio of sculpture or the craftsman's shop. The species used in construction of homes and buildings are not those generally used for wood carving and fine furniture. Dimensional lumber in sizes desired are species not to his liking. These are construction timbers of ponderosa pine, white spruce, incense cedar, Douglas fir, on occasion redwood, and sometimes oak.

If wood-carvers were to create a large demand on the wood industry, supplies of wood and development of its unique technology would be well developed. Our demands, however, are of little economic importance. Because of the small market, the large storage required, and the high cost of handling, supply centers are restricted to a few metropolitan areas. Of course, these characteristics impose high costs even when the wood is of domestic origin.

A 1969 price list from a well-known supply center gave prices on domestic and foreign woods ranging from $2.40 a board foot (144 cubic inches) to $11.70 for the following species in their respective order of value: basswood, African mahogany, Honduras mahogany, Honduras rosewood, sugar pine, cherry, American walnut, cocabola, Brazilian rosewood, and lignum vitae. The price of our American walnut was comparable to that of cocabola, and even sugar pine, a wood most often used in door- and window-framing, was priced above African and Honduras mahogany.

It may seem strange that many of our domestic species of woods are of comparable price to some of the desired exotic species. Most of the foreign woods are obtained with inexpensive labor. However, the cost of shipping and special handling makes the cost to the wood-carver often as high as our domestic woods. Our high cost is in labor from the forest operation through the milling and distribution phases.

The commercial source of wood is an artificial limitation that can be circumvented. Many species of wood are not cut commercially even for building, let alone in large dimensions. Compare the species that grow in your area with what is available at any lumberyard or sawmill. Can you find such common species as sycamore, beech, madrone, buckeye, California laurel (Oregon myrtle), Kentucky coffee tree, hackberry, American elm, etc? Why not cut, prepare, dry, and store your own flitches for your own use? There is a great variety of species and sizes to satisfy your every urge. We have not developed the domestic species that are readily available to us.

Most wood-carvers can identify perhaps a dozen species of trees, but what is this compared to the many to be seen within a day's drive of home? Become familiar with the trees of your state or province. Obtain bulletins on the subject from your state or federal agencies. Visit your local library for books on tree identification. Books on tree identification for various parts of the United States and Canada are suggested as follows: Petrides (1972) for central and eastern United States and Canada, Preston (1968) for the Rocky Mountain region, and McMinn and Maino (1951) for trees of the Pacific slope. This self-training will provide you a new awareness of your environment. It may be the first step from wood-carver and craftsman to amateur dendrologist.

If you want to experiment on wood taken from a tree you cannot identify, refer to Hough's *Encyclopedia of American Woods* (Harrar, 1957). It may be in your library. This is an encyclopedia of actual wood cuts complete with descriptions. You will find this, I am sure, a new library experience.

There are 5,000 to 6,000 vernacular names of timbers of the

world, but there are 52,000 specimens of wood of the world at the Samuel James Record Memorial Collection at Yale University (the largest in the world, Rich, 1970). This collection is not readily available to you; however, if you have a specimen of wood that cannot be identified from your own reading and study, send a sample to the Forest Products Laboratory at Madison, Wisconsin. Include information on the size of tree and where it was taken. Here, authorities and services are available to provide you an answer to the question. You will learn again the value of being a taxpayer.

Wood is where you find it. Neatly stacked piles of hardwood (figure 2) often contains species of unusual color and grain. The treetop left following the removal of veneer or peeler logs, or an old orchard that has finished its days of bearing fruit or nuts contains a gold mine for the carver. Clearings made by a bulldozer for roads and building sites often contain many worthwhile logs that the construction boss is happy to have removed. He cannot afford to waste time in cutting and transporting logs to the sawmill. This is not his business. It could be yours. Of course, one may

FIGURE 2. A winter's supply of hardwood for the fireplace, a common source of carving wood.

FIGURE 3. The supporting beams of an old barn that is being dismantled, or one that has suffered too heavy a wind or snowfall, are a source of well-dried hardwood.

purchase an entire tree outright, but this requires more time and effort. An old barn often contains beams of fine hardwoods that are well seasoned. Care must be exercised here because beams may be badly cracked or filled with nails (figure 3). The large old furniture that is no longer of value as heirlooms or functional in the home may contain well-seasoned wood for utilization in the shop. Windfalls occur during the spring and fall storms. Often these trees are free for the taking. The owner is happy to have his yard returned to its former dignified and well-kept appearance. Flotsam or driftwood offers another source which may, on occasion, be exotic. There are precautions however, that will be discussed regarding the care for tools used in cutting these logs (note end of chapter 3). I have found some excellent supplies on river bottoms after the spring floods. An ax must be a companion on these trips for testing species and quality. Pulp mills reject logs too large or crooked. These may be purchased at very small cost.

The bird pictured in the frontispiece was carved from a small walnut log taken from my winter supply of fireplace wood (figure 2). To most wood-carvers it is a desecration to use such woods as cherry, American walnut, maple, sycamore, etc., for burning. However, wherever hardwood is found, such piles of firewood are a common sight. Here is a source of wood readily available to those living in hardwood areas.

Firewood in hardwood areas is often cut from the remains of a tree originally taken for its one or two veneer logs (figure 4). The treetop and its heavy branches are then left to be salvaged as firewood. Here is one of the finest sources of wood for wood-carvers that can be found. The remains can generally be purchased from the farmer or property owner at a nominal cost. Log sections that can be cut from the top seldom exceed five feet in length. Short logs will not pay their way through the mill. Costs of special machine settings and handling make such utilization uneconomical. The wood-carver, on the other hand, can very effectively use these short lengths. He not only has the distinct advantage of purchasing such a treetop without competition, but also has the assurance of knowing there are no nails, horseshoes, barbed wire,

FIGURE 4. A black walnut treetop left for firewood after removal of the main trunk or bole for veneer or furniture lumber.

or other metallic objects embedded in the wood to destroy or greatly shorten the service length of his chain saw. One precaution: if the tree has been lying on the ground for many months, it may have serious blemishes of rot, fungus, or insect attack. Experience and reading on the subject of log defects (see chapter 7) will reduce these disappointments.

I spent an entire summer of Saturdays cutting flitches from the branchy top of a walnut tree that produced a four-foot diameter log from the first section of the top. The cost of the tree was $20; the value of the wood if purchase whold have exceeded $1,000. Two cords of firewood sold more than paid for the tree, gas, and oil for the saw and wear on the chain saw. A utility trailer used in this operation is essential for such enterprises and can be well employed with large loads of carving wood.

Renovated orchard wood gives a magnificent fire with a fine odor, little smoke, and a long burn, but is even better for wood carving. Keep an eye open for orchards that are undergoing renovation (figure 5). Apple and pear orchards grow old. Almond and English walnut orchards also need replacing. While a resident of California, I obtained the root stock of an old California English walnut orchard. The black walnut (*Juglans hindsi*) derived from the base of these trees was like Brazilian rosewood in figure and color. Some of the furniture of my house was built in the shop with that renovated orchard. If I were a resident of Hawaii, I would watch with care the renovation of a macadamia nut orchard. If the wood is half as good as the nut meats, I would happily sacrifice a week's vacation to experiment with this wood of our Pacific islands.

During vacation and local travel I find the most tempting of all the sights of a pile of logs obviously intended for burning (figure 6) or other rapid disposal. Since World War II, construction of roads, building, impoundments, etc., have lead to massive destruction of fine woods for carving and furniture. Here the eye of an experienced wood scavenger pays off. What to cut and what not to cut, what can be pulled out of the pile without physical harm to oneself or the car, what has fungus or rot, and what is free of gravel or wire. Each situation must be examined for its possibilities.

In the above circumstances the carver acts as a conservationist. The waste wood is saved for lasting beauty. Old, overmature trees, not of much value for saw timber and of no value for veneer, are a rare find for the wood-carver. These are of greatest beauty. George Nakashima, the well-known wood craftsman of New Hope, Pennsylvania, cherishes the beauty of wood from an old tree:

FIGURE 5. Renovation of an old apple orchard for new stock. In the lower view the sawyer is cutting old-yet-sound apple trees into firewood. Note the contrast of sapwood and heartwood (the darker center).

FIGURE 6. Bulldozed hardwood logs cleared in preparation of a building site.

"We like to find mature trees or even those past maturity for our work. Though young trees can be interesting in their way. An ax handle, for instance, should come from a young tree, but in older wood there is a complexity and richness of grain that can only evolve with time, a certain number of seasons and storms" (Life, 1970). These old trees give an added value in their large dimensions. A large flitch cut from a small log is more subject to cracking than one of the same size taken from a large log (see chapter 4 on cutting the flitch).

In a recent visit to Williamsburg, Virginia, the former provincial capital of Virgina, I saw what I thought was possibly the largest specimens of osage orange and persimmons in existence. Upon consulting the American Forest Association's *Social Register of 116 Big Trees* (table 1), I learned to my surprise they fell well short of the records. The January 1971 issue of *American Forests* gives the reader the common and scientific name, the circumference of the largest tree measured at four and one-half feet from the base, its height, its spread, and the location of the tree, and the nominator of the find. Inherent in this list is the information of climate and soil that indicates the maximum growth of each species. Perhaps other large representatives can be found in the same or nearby areas. Keep your eyes open.

TABLE 1
AMERICAN FOREST ASSOCIATION'S SOCIAL REGISTER OF BIG TREES[a]

SPECIES AND YEAR REPORTED	CIR.[b] AT 4½-FT.	HEIGHT	SPREAD	LOCATION OF TREE
Acacia				
Koa, *Acacia koa var. hawaiiensis* (1969)	37'4"	140'	148'	Land of Keauhou, District of Kau, Island of Hawaii
Alder				
European, *Alnus glutinosa* (1969)	5'6"	87'	32'	Berks County, Pa.
Anaqua				
Ehretia anacua (1969)	12'7"	30'	50'	Refugio, Texas
Apple				
Southern Crab, *Malus augustifolia* (1969)	4'11"	31'	36'	Orangeburg-Calhoun Tec. Center, Orangeburg, S. C.
Ash				
Black, *Fraxinus nigra* (1969)	15'3"	87'	60'	Bath, Ohio
Pumpkin,*Fraxinus pro-funda* (1969)	11'10"	109'	74'	Big Oak Tree Sate Park, Mo.
Texas, *Fraxinus texensis* (1969)	4'7"	35'	35'	Bandera County, Texas
Baccharis				
Eastern, *Baccharis halimifolia L.* (1970)	1'4"	21'	20'	Brantley Co., Ga.
Basswood				
American, *Tilia americana L.* (1969)	18'(1½')	105'	75'	Whitemarsh, Montgomery Co., Pa.
Bayberry				
Southern, *Myrica cerifera L.* (1969)	3'	28'	33'	Bradenton, Florida
Birch				
Northwestern Paper, *Betula papyrifera var. subcordata* (1970)	3'10"	65'	32'	Hell's Canyon, Adams County, Idaho
Buckeye				
Painted, *Aesculus sylvatica* (1970)	13'3"	144'	60'	Union County, Ga.
Red, *Aesculus pavia* (1968)	3'9"	33'	30'	Georgetown, S. C.
Buffaloberry				
Silver, *Shepherdia argentea* (1970)	5'6"	20'	18'	Inyo Nat. Forest, Calif.
Catalpa				
Southern, *Catalpa bignonioides* (1969)	18'5"	83'	58'	Water Valley, Miss.
Cedar				
Incense, *Libocedrus decurrens* (1969)	39'	162'		Sawyers Bay, Calif.
Port-Orford, *Chamaecyparis lawsoniana* (1968)	39'	239'	39'	Siskiyou National Forest, Coos Co., Ore.
Cherry				
Bitter, *Prunus emarginata* (1970)	5'10"	88'	33'	Lincoln County, Toledo, Ore.
Carolina Laurelcherry, *Prunus caroliniana* (1970)	10'3"	44'	47'	Dellwood, Florida
Mazzard, *Prunus avium* (1969)	19'8"	64'	62'	Philadelphia, Pa.
Chinaberry				
Melia azedarach (1970)	15'	78'	60'	Crenshaw Co., Ala.

TABLE 1
AMERICAN FOREST ASSOCIATION'S SOCIAL REGISTER OF BIG TREES[a/]

SPECIES AND YEAR REPORTED	CIR.[b/] AT 4½-FT.	HEIGHT	SPREAD	LOCATION OF TREES
Chinese Parasoltree				
Firmiana platanifolia (1969)	5'	45'	33'	Kingstree, S. C.
Chinkapin				
Allegheny, *Castanea pumila* (1970)	19'	46'	72'	Houstin County, Texas
Coconut				
Cocos nuncifera L. (1969)	3'8"	49'	21'	Clewiston, Florida
Cottonwood				
Black, *Populus trichocarpa*	30'2"	147'	97'	Unionvale, Yamhill County, Ore.
Fremont, *Populus fremontii var. fremontii* (1970)	34'10"	94'	103'	Patagonia, Arizona
Swamp, *Populus heterophylla*	16'4"	130'	120'	Richland County, S. C.
Cucumbertree				
Yellow, *Magnolia acuminata var. cordata* (1969)	10'11"	97'	65'	Longwood Gardens, Kenneth Sq. Delaware County, Pa.
Cypress				
MacNab, *Cupressus macnabiana* (1969)	5'8"	28'	37'	Magalia, Calif.
Elm				
Cedar, *Ulmus crassifolia* (1969)	15'11"	94'	70'	Bryan, Texas
Fir				
Corkbark, *Abies lasiocarpa var. arizonica* (1969)	13'9"	111'	31'	Lincoln National Forest, Ruidoso, New Mexico
Fraser, *Abies fraseri* (1969)	7'8"	78'	43'	Cashiers, N. C.
Guava				
Psidium guajava L. (1969)	2'4"	29'	35'	Bradenton, Florida
Hackberry				
Netleaf, *Celtis reticulata* (1970)	6'11"	30'	30'	Lewiston, Nez Perce County, Idaho
Hawthorn				
Birchleaf, Crataegus tortilis (1969)	3'7"	26'	15'	Morton, Grove, Ill.
Hickory				
Bitternut, *Carya cordiformis* (1970)	11'8"	133'	110'	Richland County, S. C.
Mockernut, *Carya tomentosa* (1969)	9'10"	130'	71'	Richland Parish, La
Pignut, *Carya glabra var. glabra* (1970)	15'3"	125'	87'	Brunswick, Ga.
Sand, *Carya pallida* (1969)	9'2"	93'	70'	Edgefield County, S. C.
Scarit, *Carya Xcollina* (*texana X tomentosa*) (1969)	5'11"	58'	50'	Jackson Co., Mo.
Shagbark, *Carya ovata* (1969)	13'5"	132'	80'	Senoia, Georgia
Holly				
Tawnyberry, *Ilex krugiana* (1968)	1'3"	55'	4'	Homestead, Fla.
Honeylocust				
Waterlocust, *Gleditsia aquatica* (1969)	7'7"	60'	80'	Wyndmoor, Pa.

TABLE 1

<small>AMERICAN FOREST ASSOCIATION'S SOCIAL REGISTER OF BIG TREES[a/]</small>

SPECIES AND YEAR REPORTED	CIR.[b/] AT 4½-FT.	HEIGHT	SPREAD	LOCATION OF TREE
Jerusalem-Thorn				
Parkinsonia aculeata L.	7'	36'	41'	Florence, Arizona
Juniper				
Utah, *Juniperus osteosperma* (1969)	8'7"	25'	28'	Truman Meadows, Nevada
Larch				
European, *Larix decidua* (1969)	10'5"	80'	45'	Bryn Mawr, Pa.
Locust				
Black, *Robinia pseudoacacia* L. (1969)	16'4"	103'	46'	Richmond, Mass.
Madrone				
Texas, *Arbutus texana* (1969)	5'	34'	40'	Hays County, Texas
Magnolia				
Pyramid, *Magnolia pyramidata* (1969)	6'4"	60'	37'	Newton County, Texas
Umbrella, *Magnolia tripetala* (1969)	9'8"	45'	48'	Bucks County, Pa.
Maple				
Bigleaf, *Acer macrophyllum* (1969)	25'9"	96'	94'	Polk County, Ore.
Mountain, *Acer spicatum* (1969)	7'8"	68'	62'	Weir, Kentucky
Mulberry				
Red, *Morus rubra* (1969)	17'6"	70'	75'	Gettysburg College Campus, Pa.
White, *Morus alba* (1970)	16'4"	76'	68'	St. Joseph Co., Mich.
Oak				
Bartram, *Quercus Xheterophylla* (1969)	11'9"	85'	75'	Chester County, Pa.
Bebb, *Quercus Xbebbiana* (1969)	9'2"	85'	70'	Philadelphia, Pa.
Bender, *Quercus Xbenderi* (1969)	23'10"	95'	98'	Philadelphia, Pa.
Bluejack, *Quercus incana* (1970)	6'11"	65'	55'	Newton County, Texas
Covington, *Quercus Xbyarsii* (1969)	11'8"	69'	45'	Big Oak Tree State Park, Mo.
Cherrybark, *Quercus falcata var. pagodaefolia* (1969)	24'	115'	131'	Dougherty County, Ga.
Delta Post, *Quercus stellata var. mississipiensis* (1969)	14'10"	92'	94'	Richland Parish, La.
Laurel, *Quercus laurifolia* (1969)	19'5"	102'	116'	Waycross, Ga.
Mexican Blue, *Quercus oblongifolia* (1970)	10'3" (3'11")	34'	45'	Coronado National Forest, Arizona
Oregon White, *Quercus garryana* (1970)	24'	109'	74'	Douglas County, Ore.
Overcup, *Quercus lyrata* (1969)	14'7"	126'	98'	Putnam County, Ga.
Saul, *Quercus Xsaulii*	11'11" (2'6")	85'	80'	Roslyn, Pa.
Swampwhite, *Quercus bicolor,* (1969)	21'6"	65'	80'	Luzerne County, Pa.

TABLE 1
AMERICAN FOREST ASSOCIATION'S SOCIAL REGISTER OF BIG TREES[a/]

SPECIES AND YEAR REPORTED AT 4½-FT.	CIR.[b/]	HEIGHT	SPREAD	LOCATION OF TREE
Water, *Quercus nigra* (1969)	20'11"	72'	90'	Hawkinsville, Ga.
Osage-Orange				
Maclura pomifera (1969)	23'	50'	90'	Brookneal, Va.
Paper-Mulberry				
Broussonetia papyifera (1969)	7'9"	45'	50'	Philadelphia County, Pa.
Paulownia				
Royal, *Paulownia tomentosa* (1969)	20'3"	105'	70'	Philadelphia County, Pa.
Paurotis				
Paurotis wrightii (1969)	9"	33'	3'	Bradenton, Fla.
Peppertree				
Schinus molle L. (1969)	30'	54'	75'	San Juan Capistrano, Calif.
Persimmon				
Diospyros virginiana 1969)	11'5"	51'	54'	Waterproof, La.
Pine				
Eastern White, *Pinus strobus* (1969)	18'2"	147'	73'	Blanchard, Me.
Limber, *Pinus flexilis* (1969)	28'2"	43'	36'	Little Willow Canyon, Utah
Longleaf, *Pinus palustris* (1969)	9'4"	134'	34'	Hemphill, Texas
Parry Pinyon, *Pinus quadrifolia* (1969)	3'8"	57'	15'	Delaware County, Pa.
Pitch, *Pinus rigida* (1969)	11'4"	96'	50'	Poland, Me.
Pond, *Pinus serotina* (1969)	7'3"	101'	20'	Orangeburg County, S. C.
Ponderosa, *Pinus ponderosa* (1969)	27'11"	161'	45'	Lapine, Ore.
Sand, Chocawhatchee strain *Pinus clausa* (1969)	8'7"	52'	56'	Lynn Haven, Fla.
Single-lef, *Pinus monophylla* (1969)	10'7"	31'	52'	Toiyabe National Forest, Nevada
Slash, *Pinus elliottii* (1969)	8'7"	150'	60'	Colleton County, S. C.
South Florida Slash, *Pinus elliottii var. densa* (1969)	13'	64'	64'	Sarasota, Florida
Table-Mountain, *Pinus pungens* (1969)	7'7"	75'	44'	Dahlonega, Ga.
Plum				
Chickasaw, *Prunus angustifolia* (1969)	1'10"	22'	25'	Clemson, S. C.
Hortulan, *Prunus hortulana* (1969)	2'5"	25'	29'	Van Meter State Park, Mo.
Wildgoose, *Prunus munsoniana* (1969)	4'	14'	30'	Clay County, Mo.
Poplar				
Balsam, *Populus balsamifera var. balsamifera* (1969)	13'2"	112'	59'	South Egremont, Mass.
Portiatree				
Thespesia populnea L. (1968)	7'2" (4')	28'	28'	Big Pine Key, Fla.

TABLE 1
AMERICAN FOREST ASSOCIATION'S SOCIAL REGISTER OF BIG TREES[a]

SPECIES AND YEAR REPORTED	CIR.[b] AT 4½-FT.	HEIGHT	SPREAD	LOCATION OF TREE
Possumhaw				
Ilex decidua (1970)	1'2"	25'	30'	Boggy Gut, S. C.
Prickly-Ash				
Common, *Zanthoxylum americanum* (1969)	1'4"	30'		Homochitto National Forest, Miss.
Serviceberry				
Allegheny, *Amelanchier laevis* (1970)	6'2"	60'		Silers Bald, N. C.
Silktree				
Albizia julibrissin (1969)	6'7"	60'	77'	Philadelphia, Pa.
Soapberry				
Western, *Sapindus drummondii* (1969)	6'10"	66'	55'	Newton County, Texas
Sophora				
Texas, *Sophora affinis* (1969)	4'9"	31'	30'	Real County, Texas
Spruce				
Engelmann, *Picea engelmannii* (1970)	24'2"	179'	43'	Payette Lake, Idaho
Sugarberry (Co-champions)				
Celtis laevigata (1969)	19'10"	59'	57'	North Augusta, S. C.
Celtis laevigato (1970)	11'6"	146'	108'	Richland County, S. C.
Sumac				
Smooth, *Rhus glabra* (1970)	2'4"	28'	16'	Lewiston, Idaho
Swamp Cyrilla				
Cyrilla racemiflora (1969)	1'2"	20'	15'	Berkeley County, S. C.
Sweetgum				
American, *Liquidambar styraciflua* (1970)	19'8"	125'	100'	Richland County, S. C.
Sycamore				
Arizona, *Platanus wrightii* (1969)	20'11"	90'	98'	Patagonia, Arizona
Tanoak				
Lithocarpus densiflorus (1969)	28'8"	100'	76'	Kneeland, Calif.
Torreya				
Florida, *Torreya taxifolia* (1970)	8'11"	45'	45'	Norlina, N. C.
Tupelo				
Black, *Nyssa sylvatica var. sylvatica* (1969)	16'7"	117'	69'	Harrison County, Texas
Swamp, *Nyssa sylvatica var. biflora* (1969)	8'10"	84'	62'	Miakka, Florida
Water, *Nyssa aquatica* (1970)	27'1"	105'	45'	Kinder, La.
Walnut				
Arizona, *Juglans major*	13'10" (at 2'4")	55'	63'	Nogales, Arizona
Washingtonia				
California, *Washingtonia filifera* (1969)	6'4"	41'	18'	Sarasota, Florida

TABLE 1
AMERICAN FOREST ASSOCIATION'S SOCIAL REGISTER OF BIG TREES[a]

SPECIES AND YEAR REPORTED	CIR.[b] AT 4½-FT.	HEIGHT	SPREAD	LOCATION OF TREES
Willow				
Godding, *Salix gooddingii* (1969)	24'	93'	117'	Smartsville, Calif.
Pussy, *Salix discolor* (1969)	4'5"	39'	40'	Wilmington, Mass.
Scouler, *Salix scouleriana* (1970)	5'8"	45'	20'	Valley County, Idaho
Yellow-Popular				
Liriodendron tulipifera (1969)	25'2"	135'	51'	Macon County, N. C.

[a] American Forest Association, 1971.
[b] Values in (   ) are exceptions for height of measurement.

One may desire to make a purchase of an entire tree. Under these circumstances, it may be necessary to compete with a commercial purchaser. Such a purchase is made on the basis of the main bole or trunk and/or limbs that exceed six feet in length without an interruption of branching. Here one needs to estimate the total board footage in the tree and know what the stump market prices are at that time.

The wood-carver has many advantages over the timber buyer for purchase of a tree. The first rule to remember is that the timber buyer considers the trunk or bole of the tree his lowest cost per unit of production. If this unit cost is set at one (1), then small logs are processed at twice this cost and treetops in general cost four times as much per unit of production. The timber buyer calculates what is available as one-inch, rough-sawed wood. The saw kerf leaves much of the log in sawdust. Your cuts of the log are relatively few in comparison; therefore, the calculated waste is your gain. The commercial buyer must include the high cost of labor to cut and trim the tree as well as transport it to the mill. Yours is more a labor of love. In most commercial cutting operations much of the tree top is left to rot, since the cost of handling the branched section would be excessive. The treetop, therefore, may be left as pulp wood or firewood. In this event you can more effectively compete with the pulpwood operator in the purchase of this portion of the tree.

The hand labor at the mill and kiln add greatly to the cost of one- and two-inch lumber. Each board is hand graded, stacked, and put on stickers for air drying. If the lumber is then sent to furniture maufacturers, the same lumber is regraded, resawed, redried, and repaned. Expenditures for labor in all these processes exceed the original cost of the wood. The furniture industry requires standard-length boards and standard thicknesses. Wood-carvers and crafts-men of unique furniture have no such standardization and thus gain another advantage in the purchase of wood. Until the lumber in-dustry and its technology develop less wasteful procedures, the wood-carver and craftsman stand to gain a distinct competitive advantage in the purchase of any tree.

Tables 2, 3, and 4 have been included to provide the reader a means of estimating board footage in a log or section of the tree trunk. Log measuring rule sticks about the size of a meter or yard-stick contain the information of these tables. They can be purchased from any forestry supply house. Being impressed and printed on wood they are more permanent and of greater utility under all weather conditions in the woods. If a rule stick is not used, de-termine the diameter and length of each potential log to be taken from the tree and refer to the tables mentioned above as needed to find total board feet.

If you are without the benefit of these tables, you can easily calculate the number of board feet in a log by using the Doyle log rule. To find the number of board feet in a 16-foot log according to the Doyle scale, subtract four from the diameter (in inches) of the small end of the log. Multiply the remainder by itself. This gives the contents of the log (in board feet). An 8-foot log would have half as many board feet, a 12-foot log three-fourths as many. For ex-ceptionally tall slender trees add 10 percent; for exceptionally short, stubby trees deduct 10 percent. The timber buyer has de-veloped a system for deducting board feet for log defects (crooked logs, rot, shakes, large limb knots, burls, frost cracks, lightning scars, etc.). If the log is not top quality, he will be buying far less board feet than that you calculate. For details of log defects refer to Chapter 7 and for estimating deductions in volume refer to the *National Forest Log Scaling Handbook* of the U. S. Department of Agriculture.

TABLE 2

BOARD FEET OF SAW TIMBER IN LOGS ACCORDING TO THE DOYLE LOG RULE [a/]

DIAMETER OF LOG IN INCHES OF SMALL END, INSIDE BARK	LENGTH OF LOG IN FEET										
	6	7	8	9	10	11	12	13	14	15	16
6	1	2	2	2	2	3	3	3	3	4	4
7	3	4	4	5	5	6	7	7	8	8	9
8	6	7	8	9	10	11	12	13	14	15	16
9	9	11	12	14	16	17	19	20	22	23	25
10	13	16	18	20	22	25	27	29	31	34	36
11	18	21	24	28	31	34	37	40	43	46	46
12	24	28	32	36	40	44	48	52	56	60	64
13	30	35	40	46	51	56	61	66	71	76	81
14	37	44	50	56	62	69	75	81	87	94	100
15	45	53	60	68	76	83	91	98	106	113	121
16	54	63	72	81	90	99	108	117	126	135	144
17	63	74	84	95	106	116	127	137	148	158	169
18	73	86	98	110	122	135	147	159	171	184	196
19	84	98	112	127	141	155	169	183	197	211	225
20	96	112	128	144	160	176	192	208	224	240	256
21	108	126	144	163	181	199	217	235	253	271	289
22	121	142	162	182	202	223	243	263	283	304	324
23	135	158	180	203	226	248	271	293	316	338	361
24	150	175	200	225	250	275	300	325	350	375	400
25	165	193	220	248	276	303	331	358	386	413	441
26	181	212	242	272	302	333	363	393	423	454	484
27	198	231	264	298	331	364	397	430	463	496	529
28	216	252	288	324	360	396	432	468	504	540	576
29	234	273	312	352	391	430	469	508	547	586	625
30	253	296	338	380	422	465	507	549	591	634	676
31	273	319	364	410	456	501	547	592	638	683	729
32	294	343	292	441	490	539	588	636	686	735	784
33	315	368	420	473	526	578	631	683	736	788	841
34	337	394	450	506	562	619	675	731	787	844	900
35	360	420	480	541	601	661	721	781	841	901	961
36	384	448	512	576	640	704	768	832	896	960	1,024
37	408	476	544	613	681	749	817	885	953	1,021	1,089
38	433	506	578	650	722	795	867	939	1,011	1,084	1,156
39	459	536	612	689	766	842	919	995	1,072	1,148	1,225
40	486	567	648	729	810	891	972	1,053	1,134	1,215	1,296

SOURCE: *Trees* Yearbook of Agriculture. U.S. Dept. Agric., 1949.

[a] To find the number of board feet in a 16-foot log according to the Doyle scale, subtract 4 from the diameter (in inches) of the small end of the log. Multiply the remainder by itself. This gives the contents of the log (in board feet). An 8-foot log would have half as many board feet, a 12-foot log three-fourths as many.

A section of a walnut tree that occupied a fence line.

A supply of hardwood for the fireplace, a common source of carving wood.

Flitches of four hardwood species, labeled with size and weight at each month of **weighing.**

TABLE 3

BOARD FEET OF SAW TIMBER IN TREES ACCORDING TO INTERNATIONAL ¼-INCH RULE

DIAMETER OF TREE IN INCHES 4.5 FEET ABOVE GROUND LEVEL	NUMBER OF 16-FOOT LOGS				
	1	1½	2	2½	3
10	39	51	63	72	80
11	49	64	80	92	104
12	59	78	98	112	127
13	71	96	120	138	156
14	83	112	141	164	186
15	98	132	166	194	221
16	112	151	190	223	256
17	128	174	219	258	296
18	144	196	248	292	336
19	162	222	281	332	382
20	181	248	314	370	427
21	201	276	350	414	478
22	221	304	387	458	528
23	244	336	428	507	586
24	266	368	469	556	644
25	290	402	514	610	706
26	315	436	558	662	767
27	341	474	606	721	836
28	367	510	654	779	904
29	396	551	706	842	977
30	424	591	758	904	1,050
31	454	634	814	973	1,132
32	485	678	870	1,042	1,213
33	518	724	930	1,114	1,298
34	550	770	989	1,186	1,383
35	585	820	1,055	1,266	1,477
36	620	870	1,121	1,346	1,571
37	656	922	1,188	1,430	1,672
38	693	974	1,256	1,514	1,772
39	732	1,031	1,330	1,602	1,874
40	770	1,086	1,403	1,690	1,977

SOURCE: *Trees* Yearbook of Agriculture. U.S. Dept. Agric., 1949.

TABLE 4

BOARD FEET OF SAW TIMBER IN TREES ACCORDING TO DOYLE LOG RULE

DIAMETER OF TREE IN INCHES 4.5 FEET ABOVE GROUND LEVEL	NUMBER OF 16-FOOT LOGS				
	1	1½	2	2½	3
10	16	20	23	24	26
11	24	30	35	38	42
12	31	39	47	52	57
13	42	53	64	72	80
14	52	67	82	93	104
15	64	84	104	118	132
16	77	101	125	143	161
17	92	122	152	175	198
18	108	144	179	206	234
19	126	168	210	244	278
20	144	193	242	282	321
21	164	221	278	324	370
22	185	250	315	368	420
23	208	282	356	417	478
24	231	314	397	466	536
25	256	350	443	522	600
26	282	386	489	576	663
27	310	425	540	638	735
28	339	466	592	700	807
29	370	509	648	766	884
30	400	552	703	832	961
31	434	599	764	906	1,049
32	467	646	824	980	1,137
33	502	696	889	1,060	1,230
34	538	746	954	1,138	1,322
35	576	801	1,026	1,225	1,424
36	615	857	1,099	1,312	1,526
37	656	915	1,174	1,406	1,638
38	697	973	1,249	1,499	1,749
39	740	1,036	1,332	1,598	1,864
40	784	1,099	1,414	1,696	1,979

SOURCE: *Trees* Yearbook of Agriculture. U.S. Dept. Agric., 1949.

[a] For exceptionally tall, slender trees add 10 percent. For exceptionally short, stubby trees deduct 10 percent.

Learn what the current stumpage value is and hedge your offer above the value. Remember your advantages as outlined above. Stumpage value, i.e., the value per thousand feet in a standing tree, represents a fifth to a tenth that purchased as sawed at the mill or speciality supply house. Current stumpage values can be obtained from your state forester. Give him a call and compare the values he gives for different grades with what they are at the mills or speciality shops. The range of these values reflects differences in the quality of the wood and differences in handling and selection.

The wood-carver or craftsman can utilize wood in his area for minimal cost at his convenience and at sizes and quality he determines by his own selection and cutting. He can experiment with many species, some of which cannot be purchased even from speciality shops. With experience, he learns a joy of artistry that begins with the tree and ends with the final form.

If even a greater range of experience is desired, why not utilize the information in this book and trade flitches of different species with fellow wood-carvers and craftsmen in other parts of the country or even the world? As a starter I would suggest using the National Wood-Carver's Association list of members for making such contacts. As you become familiar with each wood, cut a representative one-piece sample for your reference library of woods. Hang it with those samples of other species from a brass eyehook in your shop. Learn to identify your wood through more than superficial appearance. The character of the cells of each species of wood are as distinctive as the character of faces of all mankind. Just a difference in the vessel size and distribution in hardwoods produces distinct differences in texture and figure when carved. Species of hardwood with vessels most conspicuous (large vessels) in the early wood of the annual rings are ring-porous. The pores that can be observed with the naked eye in some species or viewed with the help of a hand lens in other species are the water-conducting vessels. The figure is bold (figure 7). If the species is semi-ring-porous, i.e., the conspicuous vessels occur in the early wood and somewhat in the late wood, the figure is more subtle (figure 8). On the other hand, the figure of diffuse-porous wood must depend upon other factors for beauty. The vessels are distributed throughout the early and late wood (figure 9).

The arrangement of vessels in the woods of broad-leaved trees identify the three major types of "hardwood" of the broad-leaved

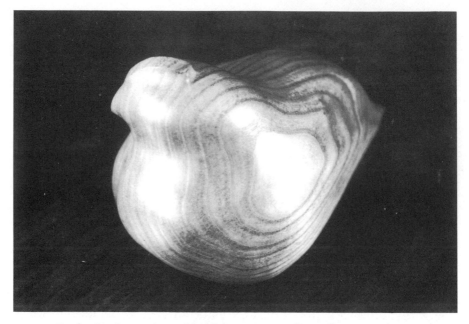

FIGURE 7. Author's carving of bird from Kentucky coffee tree, a ring-porous wood that gives bold figure. Carving measures 4½″ x 5½″ x 9″.

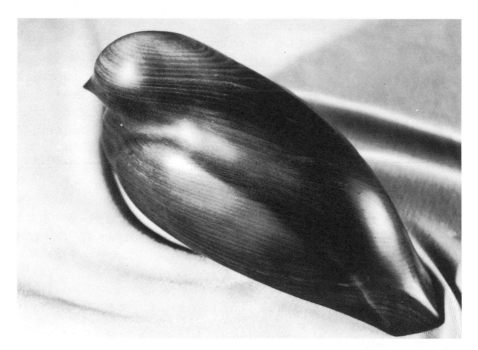

FIGURE 8. Author's carving of a bird in American black walnut, a semi-ring-porous wood. Note the top knot of sapwood. Carving measures 5″ x 6″ x10″

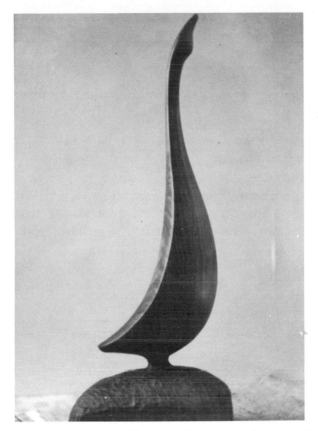

FIGURE 9. *Upper*: Carving of a goose from wild black cherry, a diffuse-porous wood. Wood figure is more subtle than that of vessel type noted in figures 7 and 8. The flitch prior to carving measured 6″ x 9″ x 22″. (Courtesy of wood-carver Maurice Ganter, Mechanicsville, Pennsylvania). *Lower*: Author's carving of a wolf in wild black cherry. Note the crotch figure along the ruff of the neck. The carving measures 6″ x 6½″ x 10½″.

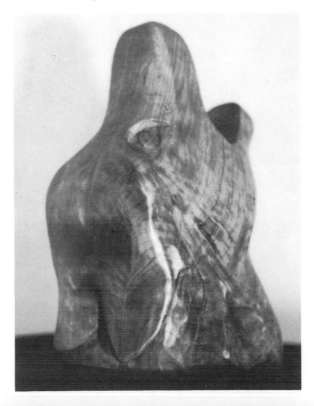

species. Structures of similar function in the conifers are tracheids. They are elongate, thin-walled cells in the early wood. In the late wood they are heavy walled and provide support to the tree's growth of these "softwood" species. These cells are about 3.5 mm long (about 100 x the diameter). The vessels of the broad-leaved trees and the tracheids of the conifers (figure 10) perform the function of conduction of water from the roots (table 5). Heavy walled tracheids in the late wood provide support in the conifers, whereas, fiber tracheids (thick cell walls) in the broad-leaved trees provide support for these species.

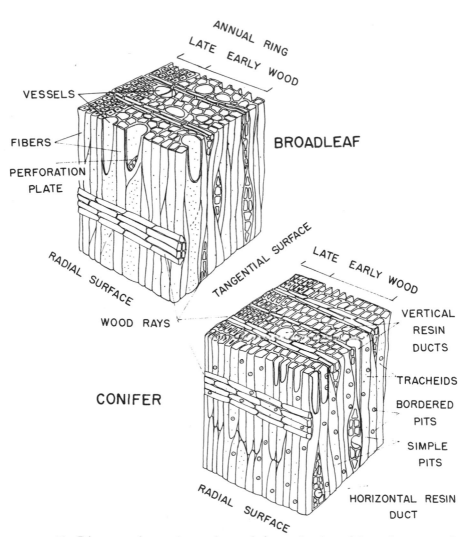

FIGURE 10. Diagramatic sections of wood from the broad-leaved trees and the conifers. These features can be seen with a 10 to 20X power hand lens.

Those familiar with conifers of the South know well the hardness of coniferous wood and how soft some broad-leaved species (e.g. basswood) are. The terms "hardwood" and "softwood", therefore, are very confusing and for this reason it is best to refer to the two different types of cellular structure as coming from broad-leaved trees and conifers respectively.

Radial transfer of materials and food storage occurs in the rays of both conifers and broad-leaved trees. These are thin-celled, bricklike structures that radiate in continuous development from year to year from the pith outward. They remain the live cells in sapwood. Resin canals present in may of the conifers (table 5) are not found in any of the broad-leaved trees. Pits are well developed tracheid structures in the conifers through which water and materials in solution are passed from cell to cell. The pits in fiber tracheids of the broad-leaved trees are usually smaller and often simpler in structure.

TABLE 5

STRUCTURE AND FUNCTIONAL FEATURES OF CONIFERS ("SOFTWOODS")
AND BROADLEAVED ("HARDWOOD") TREES

FUNCTION	CONIFERS	BROADLEAVED
Conduction of water and materials from roots	Tracheids of early (thin-walled) and late wood.	Vessels: ring-porous to diffuse-porous. Are thin-walled cells
Support	Tracheids of late wood (compact and dense). Tracheids about 3.5 mm. long (100 x cross section diameter). Pointed at end and with a myriad pits	Fiber tracheids (compact and dense)
Passage of fluids from cell to cell	Pits through which water and materials in solution pass	Pits are smaller and generally simpler in structure
Radial transfer of materials and food storage	Rays: bricklike thin-walled structures. Remain live cells in sapwood	Rays are same as conifers
Secretion and movement of resin	Resin canals (pines, spruces, larches, and Douglas Fir)	Resin canals are absent
Block passage of fluids	Tyloses not in all species	Tyloses not in all species
Growth center for increase in stem, branch, and twig diameter	Cambium cells: produces tracheid cells, ray structures, resin canals, and phloem. Phloem for transfer of food from needles	Same as conifers: produces vessels, fiber tracheids, ray structures, and phloem. Phloem for transfer of food from leaves
Replacement of tissue to outside of tree	Cork cambium exterior to above phloem tissue	Same as conifers

Tyloses, balloonlike growths that develop from a live cell into another cell through pits, are found in some but not all species of both types. Tyloses block the conduction of sap in the sapwood or develop from sapwood into the adjacent cells of heartwood.

Cambium, the growth center that provides for increase in diameter of stems, limbs, and twigs, is common in both conifer and broad-leaved species. This is a paper-thin layer of cells that produce to the interior the early and late wood in both types of trees. Likewise, phloem cells are produced to the exterior from the cambium Phloem tissue conducts food from the photosynthesizing tissues of the trees for storage in other parts of the tree structure. Cork cambium occurs on both conifers and broad-leaved trees outside phloem tissues. The cells produced from the cork cambium are to the outside of the tree and in time are sloughed off. Cork or bark cells produced at one time do not remain a permanent part of the wood structure in either the conifers or broad-leaved species. For practical implications note figure 44 and the related discussion in chapter 7.

In the conifers, heartwood and sapwood are commonly distinct. The heartwood in both conifers and broad-leaved species generally becomes darker in color. Figure (note table 11 and related discussion of chapter 9) of conifer wood, therefore, is primarily made up of color differences between the heartwood and sapwood and

FIGURE 11. Carving of eagle from lamination of two pieces of white pine. The larger piece (excluding the head and upper wing margins) came from a 125-year-old structure that housed drovers and drivers who worked the old Pennsylvania turnpike in the Boalsburg, Pennsylvania, area. Note the figure on the head. The carving measures 6″ x 24″ x 55″. (Courtesy of wood-carver Nelson Wood of Boalsburg, Pennsylvania)

differences in the density of tissues laid down as early wood and late wood. Figure is less pronounced in the conifers (the southern pines are exceptions) than in the broad-leaved species (figure 11).

For a more thorough understanding and appreciation of these two types of wood, refer to *Inside Wood, Masterpiece of Nature* by William M. Harlow (1970) and to Panshin and Zeeuw (1970).

2

Tools For Cutting the Flitch

Either the wood-carver and craftsman must continue to expend considerable sums of money to purchase wood or he should make a long-term investment in equipment to cut and handle his own supply. I have found the following equipment to serve my needs in all circumstances: The peavey (figure 12, A) is used to roll a log into position prior to cutting (note end of chapter 3) or to turn any portion of tree for more convenient cutting. Wedges (figure 12, B) will be needed on many occasions to direct the falling of a tree soon after the undercut is made. These may also be used to split log sections too large to saw. Also, wedges are used to prevent wood from pinching the saw blade. Wedges rather than the chain saw, should always be used to split logs that may contain rocks or metal. Wedges of aluminum alloy, although slightly more expensive than steel, are much less damaging to the chain saw when there is a high probability of saw-wedge contact. A third tool, the splitting maul (figure 12, C), should be used to assist all log-splitting operations. A sharp ax is always a necessity in tree work. Although the previous items are relatively inexpensive, the most expensive and the most personal item is the chain saw (figure 12, D).

The chain saw should be adequately powered, since many cuts are made with the lower cutting edge fully employed in cutting parallel to the long axis of the tree. My saw is a seven-horsepower unit that handles well the two bars and two chains, either pair which may be attached to the power unit. An 18-inch bar can be used with ease to divide a 15-inch log, but cannot slab an 18-inch log in one cut. The chain is inefficient in cutting perpendicular to the end surface of a log. Logs of a diameter greater than bar length may be split with two cuts on either side and hopefully in the same plane

FIGURE 12. Equipment used in cutting tree to log to flitch. A is a peavey, B is an aluminum wedge, C is a splitting maul, and D is the chain saw with an 18-inch bar and chain in foreground for use on small timber.

(figure 13). This takes some practice but can be mastered in time. It is convenient to have a 36-inch saw bar to handle, in one slice, logs 18 to 25 inches in diameter. A few of our West Coast colleagues will find need of a larger saw for the redwood logs found on beaches and river beds. Equipment that should be with the chain saw, of course, is a gas can specifically for the gas-oil mix.

A filing set that includes a guide and file should be used frequently (figure 14) to maintain the chippers and rakers of the chain in top condition. Match the file to the size of the chippers. File in only one direction so as to prolong the service life of the file. Use the same number of strokes on each chipper to maintain even wear on the chippers. Chippers are like teeth on a saw. If one side of the chain contains sharper chippers than the other, the saw will pull in a curving cut to the sharp side. Sharp chippers coupled with adequate oiling throughout the cutting operation will reduce effort required, increase precision of cutting, and prolong the life of the saw. If the chippers are dull and oil is used sparingly, the stresses placed upon the saw will cause excessive wear on the bar

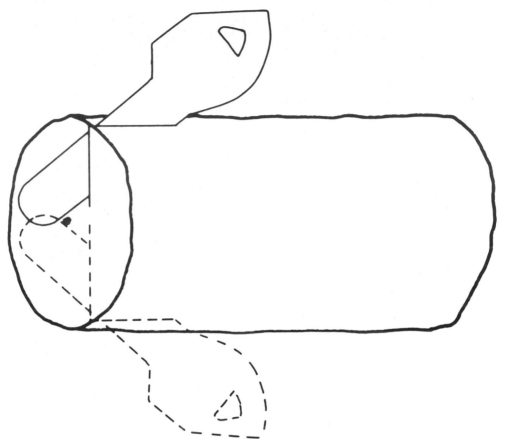

FIGURE 13. Use of chain saw to section log with diameter too great to be cut in one slice.

and chain as well as strain on the engine. Keep the chippers sharp. For further details refer to instructions received with your saw or write the manufacturer for details—don't spare the oil.

A mason's chalk line is of great help in marking a cut parallel to the axis of the tree (figure 15) that exceeds the length of the saw blade. By placing the cotton cord well filled with chalk at the proposed line of cut and snapping it smartly against the length of the log, one gets a straight, well-defined line, a guide for cutting the flitches and billets (see chapter 4).

FIGURE 14. One type of filling set used to maintain a fine cutting edge. The device guides the operator for correct depth and angle of cut with the file.

FIGURE 15. A mason's chalk line is used to mark a cutting line for logs that exceed the length of the chain saw. The chalk line is held tight, pulled straight from the log, and released sharply against it. Chalk is deposited from the line at all points of contact.

The final items of equipment, though not pictured, are necessary for survival: the hard hat and ear protectors. In the following chapter on felling trees the utility of the hard hat will become apparent. Good carving and craftsmanship require an intact brain.

Also, you must retain your hearing to enjoy the resonance of wood and detect defects in the log and flitches by noting the firmness of sound upon striking a large piece. Protect the ears. Purchase ear protectors from a gun store or an industrial supply house. Prices range from 7 to 10 dollars.

In the October 1972 issue of *Consumer Reports,* 19 gasoline-powered chain saws were tested for noise. Even the quietest model was noisy enough to threaten permanent damage to one's hearing. One model tested put out a truly ear-shattering 117 decibels when cutting. Even a fifteen-minute exposure to such a noise level could permanently damage hearing. Several other saws cut at about 110 d, enough noise to pose a threat to hearing after about half an hour.

3

Felling a Tree

If you are an inveterate wood scavenger, your finds for the most part will be of logs and trees lying on the ground. However, there may come the occasion when you purchase a living tree—hopefully one that is past maturity and is soon to die or one that will soon be eliminated as a result of "man's progress." To cover all aspects of wood-carver's syndrome, I shall start with the cutting of the living tree and end with the final cutting of desirable flitches.

Of course a tree may be cut at any time, but there are advantages and disadvantages for cutting different times of the year. To cut in the winter or fall because "the sap is down" may be the correct time for several reasons, but certainly not for this reason. Anyone that has witnessed the frost splitting a tree when temperatures reach 25 to 35 below zero knows that this is the result of sap within the trunk freezing, expanding, and bursting the cellular structure. Sap is in the roots, trunk, and limbs of the tree at all seasons of the year.

Late fall or early winter are the best times to cut a tree. The temperatures inhibit the growth of wood destroying fungi. Warm temperatures and high humidity in late spring and summer are optimal for the growth of fungus (refer to chapter 8). Another advantage at this time of the year, not commonly appreciated, is the freedom from wood-borer infestation. Wood-boring insects seem to detect readily a weakened tree or a recently cut tree and proceed during the early spring and summer breeding periods to fill the inner bark, cambium, and sapwood with eggs of their species. It is a depressing experience to learn that a carefully chosen flitch has been badly infested with wood-boring insects.

Cutting a tree in the spring has been suggested and is practiced by some. This is the poorest time to cut a tree. It has been assumed

47

that one should cut at the time of budding so as to permit the cut tree to send forth its leaves and exhaust the moisture in the live part of the tree, the sapwood. Of course, the leaves will appear and through normal transpiration processes quickly wilt. It is assumed that the wilting is the result of the unbound moisture in the sapwood being transpired. The loss of water, however, is only local. There is no loss of moisture from the wood.

Regardless of when the cutting is done, there are some pre-liminaries that should be considered so as to save your equipment, every potential piece of carving wood, nearby buildings or struc-tures, and perhaps even your life. How sound is the tree? Are there any large, rotten branches? If so, use caution, for the tree may have a rotten center. These branches and others that extend awkwardly from the main trunk should be removed prior to felling. Rotten branches, if left attached, scatter over the area at the moment of impact. Your hard hat should be worn at all times to insure against injury under these circumstances.

Large, sound limbs should be removed prior to felling if possible. In removing these after the tree is on the ground you may find them under heavy stress. Sudden release of these stresses with the chain saw may cause injury to the sawyer. Furthermore, the break-ing of sound limbs destroys potentially good carving wood at the juncture with the main trunk.

Examine the position of the tree in the field, or wherever it is located, to obtain some idea whether or not the tree formerly oc-curred in a fence row or was used to support other than its own structure. It was a common practice in the past and remains so to-day that trees along fence rows support barbed wire and other types of cattle fencing. They become embedded in the tree's growth and, if struck with the saw, seriously shorten the service life of the chain or the power saw. Some hints of the presence of wire, staples, or on occasion horseshoes can be noted in the callous growth of bark. If the texture of the bark near the base of the tree trunk shows irregular patterns of bark arrangement, there is good reason to suspect embedded materials in the wood that have been subsequent-ly enclosed with living tissue (note further discussion of this in chapter 7). An example of callous growth and stained wood caused by embedded iron can be seen in figure 16. It is wise to debark such areas with the ax prior to application of chain saw. If in doubt, cut well above the fence line or very close to the ground.

Before making the first cut, determine the direction of the lean of the tree itself. This is done very simply with the use of a plumb line

FIGURE 16. A section of a walnut tree that occupied a fence line. The callous growth of the inner bark can be seen at the top of the picture. External strands of barbed wire and the embedded staples can be identified indirectly with the black iron-staining of wood. Only wedges and the splitting maul should be used to prepare flitches from logs of this condition.

held with arm extended and visually superimposed on the tree trunk while standing some 25 to 50 feet from the base of the tree. With such viewing from a complete circle of the tree, one can observe at wihch position the tree diverges maximally from the linc of plumb.

It is here that the first cut parallel to the ground is made (1 of figure 17). Cut 1 should be far enough above ground to allow completion of the undercut 2. While cut 1 is made, watch carefully to observe the firmness of the wood that is ejected by the chain saw. If the wood appears firm and has an odor of freshness, proceed with a cut into approximately ⅓ the diameter of the tree. If there is any indication that the color of the wood is dark and is accompanied with softness and a distinctly sour or rotten wood smell, proceed with caution. There may not be sufficient tree structure to support the tree and to keep its shift in position from pinching your saw. To reduce possibilities of pinching, I make the practice of using a slicing withdrawal action on cut 1 at all times. In the event the tree begins to pinch, I can rapidly withdraw the bar. This

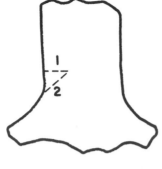

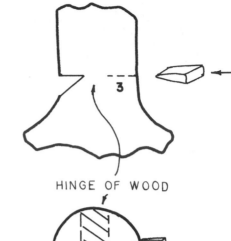

HINGE OF WOOD

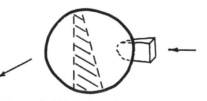
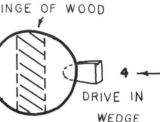

DRIVE IN
WEDGE

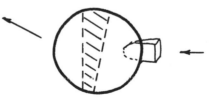

DIRECTION OF FALL   SHAPE OF HINGE

FIGURE 17. Steps in felling a tree in the direction of its natural lean.

facility comes with some practice and experience.

One can proceed with cut 3 in the same plane as cut 1 following completion of the undercut. As the saw proceeds in cut 3, note the change in position of the very top of the tree. A slight change at the cut will make a large change in the top. If the top begins to move in the direction of the undercut, the saw should be withdrawn and the operator should move back in a position perpendicular to the plane of falling. In the event the tree drops quickly, the operator is then not in a position to receive the kickback of the tree trunk once it breaks away from the hinge.

Sometimes the tree may remain standing even when a third of the trunk has been cut through on the third operation. This is a safe time to withdraw the chain saw and apply a steel wedge as step 4. The wedge can be driven in with the splitting maul and the tree tilted on its stump to a critical position of falling. Once falling begins, the operator removes himself in the same manner as above. On occasion, one may desire to fell the tree slightly off the direction of its natural lean. This operation may be effected by leaving a heavier hinge of uncut wood on the side in which the tree should be tilted. This off-center felling is brought about by the falling tree in breaking the hinge first on its narrowest portion. The thicker-hinged portion then acts to pull the tree to that portion of the stump as it drops to the ground (figure 17).

There are times when a tree has to be dropped against the direction of its natural lean. The tree may overhang a wall, building, or simply be inconvenient to process if dropped in the direction of its natural lean. Under these circumstances, there are special procedures that must be followed. The basic practice involved in this operation is that the wedge, an incline plane, must be used to move the tree gradually from its natural tilt to one of tilt in the opposite direction

Unfortunately, the limbing process practiced in the previous type of felling should not be carried out except on the side of the natural lean. All branches on the opposite side should be left intact to provide additional weight and leverage to assist movement of the tree against its natural falling position.

The first cut is made close to the base and parallel to the ground. It is made on the side with the natural lean and is cut something less than a third the diameter of the tree. Prior to making the undercut of step 3 and 4 (figure 18), an aluminum wedge is driven well into the cut (step 2, figure 18). The wedge is driven at a slight angle so as to allow room for subsequent cutting with the chain saw noted in step 5. The undercut of 3 and 4 is made the usual one third of the diameter. These proportions of the trunk are based on the assumption that the tree trunk has shown no evidence of inner or other weaknesses. One would be well advised before proceeding with any cutting to check the soundness of the tree by making an increment boring with brace and bit. If there are any inner weaknesses (hollowness or rotten wood), make the undercut less than one-third the trunk's diameter.

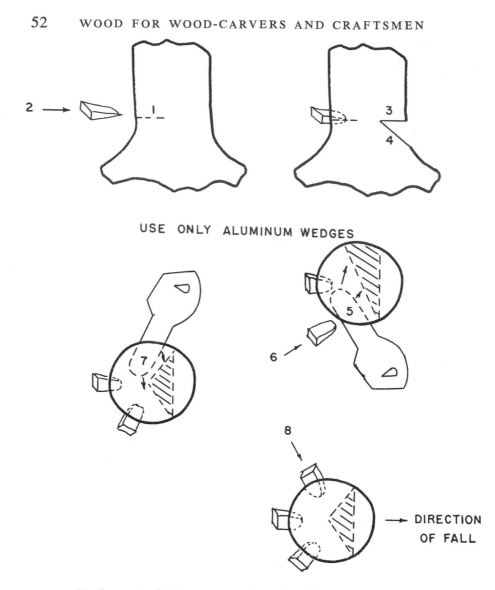

FIGURE 18. Steps in felling tree against the direction or opposite to its natural lean. Inserting of the wedge in step 6 follows cutting with the saw and its removal, Step 5.

The chain saw is used to deepen the cut made at site 1 (noted as step 5, figure 18) following completion of the undercut. Under the conditions of this cut there is some likelihood of wedge-chain saw contact. Chances of damaging the chain saw at this time are greatly reduced if aluminum rather than steel wedges are used. Once the cut is completed in step 5, an aluminum wedge is driven into that portion of the second cut (step 6). When the operator has position-ed the two aluminum wedges firmly in place, the chain saw is then taken to the opposite side of the bole or trunk of the tree and a cut is made as noted in step 7. An aluminum wedge is driven in as step 8 when this cut is completed. The hinge of wood now left connected to the main trunk of the tree is triangular in shape and remains as the supporting structure balanced on three wedges. At this stage, if the treetop can be moved toward the direction of intended fall with subsequent tapping of wedges at 2, 6, and 8, steel wedges can be inserted in the saw kerf and driven in with much greater force. As the tree begins to move in the direction of its planned fall, the wedges are driven in farther until the center of gravity shifts causing the tree to fall in the direction opposite the lean.

To keep your peace of mind and to save my conscience, please practice this latter falling operation in an open area many times to gain confidence and experience for this risky task. As a safety factor, I have used a heavy line tied to as near the sturdy top of the tree as possible and anchored to the base of a nearby tree in the direction of intended fall. A block-and-tackle or "come-along" may be used on the main line near the base of the anchor tree to maintain a continuous mechanical advantage throughout the operation. Better yet, a line tied midway to this rope and kept under continuous ten-sion with a car or block-and-tackle system offers an extremely high mechanical advantage in toppling the tree in the direction intended.

I should hope that your first tree arrives on the ground without injury to you, your equipment, animals, or fellow human beings. Now is the time to remove the other limbs from the main trunk. Those limbs free of weight of the tree and other structures should be removed first starting with the top of the tree and the tops of each free limb. Limbs under tension from support of the trunk and other tree structures should be left uncut at this time. As one moves down from the top to the base of the tree, limbs should be removed that balance all parts of the tree. Always stand on the side away from the limb being cut. This procedure avoids the danger of having the tree turn from release of a heavy, single limb. Remember to wear your hard hat. If such danger is imminent, that limb should be treated in the same manner as the tree itself. Begin by removing small branches from its top and work toward the tree trunk.

Once all free branches are removed, an attempt should be made to turn the tree with the peavey. However, if it cannot be turned and limbs under the weight of the tree trunk have to be removed, the first cut of each limb after debranching should be made on the

FIGURE 19. Use of the peavey to roll a log onto supporting timbers. The log is rolled in the direction of the pike on the peavey.

side of greatest tension. Be careful to avoid the sudden splitting and springing of wood when undertaking this cut. Attempt, after the removal of each of these large, supporting limbs, to turn the tree so as to reduce as much as possible the need to cut limbs under extreme tension.

The major limbs and tree trunk itself are now on the ground and free of all limb structures. Each of the sections can be turned with one or two men using peaveys as illustrated in figure 19. Roll the log onto large timbers or smaller log supports to elevate them above the ground. The log perched above the ground can be examined more easily for cutting. It can be cut with less damage to the saw. Of special importance, fungi in the soil are far less likely to invade the log in this position. Flitch and billet (note chapter 4) as soon as possible after felling to minimize fungal development and checking.

The log may have been cut some time ago. You may have found it on the river bottom or shore as flotsam. This, too, should be rolled upon large timbers for examination of knots, metal, and especially at these sites, sand. Sand contains quartz, a very hard mineral that rapidly dulls the chain. Brush the area that is to be cut vigorously with a wire brush, or use an ax to cut away the surface lines of cut. By all means avoid sand-saw contact.

4

Cutting the Flitch

Another aspect of "wood-carver's syndrome" is the anxious period of anticipation before opening a log section to view for the first time the quality of the interior wood. Questions that come to the mind are: What will I get for my time, effort, and expenditures? What is the diversity of figure in the wood? Are there any blemishes, shakes, or stains? Is the wood rotten? Is the log section free of insect infestation? Are there some hidden stubs or worse yet, metal?

Hopefully the job can be completed without damage to the saw. Prior to making any cuts, the log section should be observed carefully to note any indication of wire, nails (figure 16), horseshoes, chain, and other farm equipment often left hanging in the low crotches of what was formerly a sapling (note chapter 7 of log defects). If there is any reason for questioning the condition of the area to be cut, it should be debarked with an ax and examined. If still in doubt, use the wedges and maul for splitting. Do not risk damage to the saw.

If the log has been cut for some time, the ends may be badly checked in the pith area. Heart checks develop from the pith if the log has been exposed to drying. Remove a five- to six-inch section of the checked ends (figure 20).

Roll the log with the peavey and examine all surfaces to determine where cuts should be made that will maximize usage of carving wood and minimize waste. The sections or bolts cut should be those that can be handled or stored with ease. Unless I have something large in mind, I cut bolts just short of the length of the bar (figures 21 and 22). Once the log has been cut into bolts, each should be rolled upon timbers well above the ground. Here final

FIGURE 20. Removing the end section of a log that has dried and cracked to form heart checks.

FIGURE 21. Cutting the log into bolts for convenience of handling, slabbing and carving. The length of the bolt desired here is marked on the peavey handle and at two places on the log.

FIGURE 22. A section of log being cut after removal of end with heart checks. The darkened area of the outer left circumference has been invaded with stain and fungi and will be removed as planned in figure 26. On methods to avoid the development of fungi refer to chapter 8.

inspection can be made for marking prior to cutting the flitches.

Optimal utilization of the bolt depends upon an understanding of the drying process and of abnormal growth defects (note chapters 6 and 7). Let us depart for a moment from the cutting of flitches to principles that should be employed to make decisions as to where the cuts should be made. Most often I prepare four flitches (A, B, C, and D, figure 23) from a symmetrical log. A and C flitches are more properly referred to as billets. In the early period of American history these sections of the log cut from oak were termed wainscot billets. They were shipped in this form; later cut as planks along the lesser dimension for wainscotting in home construction. At that time wainscot billets were generally of oak and presented figure that highlighted the medullary rays. The center planks of the billet were of "quarter-sawed" figure, a cut that maximized exposure of the rays. This cut, more appropriately termed radial sawed is

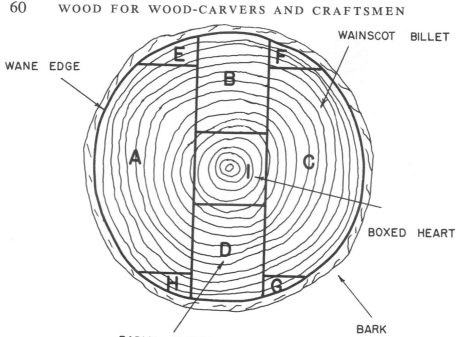

FIGURE 23. Diagram of flitches (A through H) that should be cut from a log without defects. Wainscot billets (A and C) are for large carvings; flitches B and D are radially sawed but smaller flitches; and E through H are of least value. The heart with pith (I) should be "boxed out" (discarded). It is a section highly susceptible to checking.

obtained in flitches B and D of figure 23. The flitches E, F, G, and H may be saved for small carvings, but these are often discarded, since the annual ring structure does not give a balanced figure. Furthermore, the proportion of sapwood to heartwood is much greater. For large carvings, the billets A and C are most desirable. However, flitches B and D have much greater stability from cracking and checking during the drying process. Billets A and C have the best figure and, if knots are present, they can be incorporated more readily in carving than in the flitches B and D. The knots appear round instead of spikelike as developed in the radial-sawed flitches B and D.

The billets are considered tangential or plane sawed, which accounts for their more symmetric and interesting wood figure. Where simple figure is desired flitches B and D are to be preferred. Each flitch has its advantage from the standpoint of drying, stability, beauty, etc. (table 6).

TABLE 6

ADVANTAGES AND DISADVANTAGES OF RADIAL- AND TANGENTIAL-SAWED WOOD

Radial or Quarter-Sawed	*Tangential or Plain-Sawed*
1. Best figure is obtained with those species having well developed medullary rays over annual ring development (sycamore, mahogany, oak, etc.). Oak has well developed rays but also well developed annual rings. Figure therefore can be developed by either plain or quarter sawing; however, there is a different figure in each cut.	1. Best figure is generally obtained because contrast of texure, grain and color are maximized.
2. Shrinks less because annual rings have minimum circumferential distance relationship to size of block.	2. It dries more rapidly than quarter sawed blocks of same dimension under the same condition. Flitches of this cut must be watched to avoid surface checking.
3. Twists and cups less because the variability or unevenness of annual rings is less expressed in this cut.	3. It does not collapse (water loss in cells plus tension of cell walls cause inner wood cells to collapse) as readily as quarter-sawed flitches of the same size.
4. Does not surface check so badly in air drying, therefore, can be dried with more rapid drop in humidity.	4. If knots are present they can be incorporated more readily in carving, since they are round instead of spike knots as develoved in radial sawed flitches.
5. Is easier to cut and sand. Less development of slivers.	

The rule of thumb or principle that must be remembered in planning the cutting of the log into flitches is that the greater the ratio of length of the longest annual ring in cross section to the thickness of the flitch, the greater the danger of cracking. This is more traditionally expressed in wood technology as the differential between tangential and radial shrinkage. The former perspective is much more realistic, particularly so when flitches are to be used for carving in the round (note chapter 6).

Take advantage as often as possitble of the asymmetry in the log. Design the cuts of the log in preparation of the flitch to include the portion containing the least curvature in the annual ring formation. In figure 24, A the log is cut into two billets of plane-sawed wood and two flitches of radial-sawed wood. The billets include that section of the log with the least curvature in the annual rings. Such a billet will not suffer as much cracking as one whose cut includes annual rings with great curvature or length of annual rings to thickness of flitch (figure 24, C). The differential in shrinkage of

FIGURE 24. Principles illustrated for cutting flitches from an asymmetric log.

A

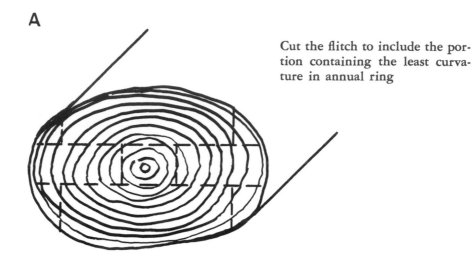

Cut the flitch to include the portion containing the least curvature in annual ring

B

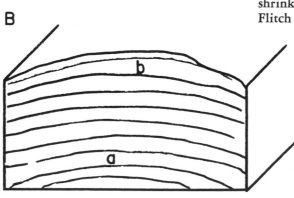

Flitch with low diffenential shrinkage between areas a and b. Flitch from a large tree

C

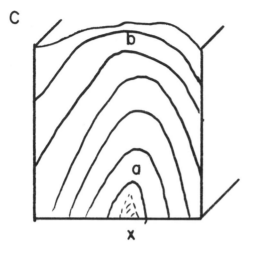

Flitch with much differential shrinkage between areas a and b. Checking and cracking maximized at x. Refer to section on reaction wood

D

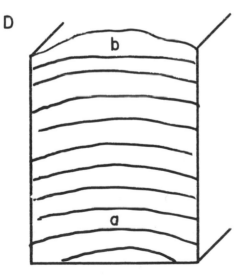

Radial flitch with least differential shrinkage. Areas a and b similar in potential shrinkage

cells around the annual ring *a* versus that around the annual ring *b* is so great as to cause splitting or cracking in the area most closely related to the center of the log. This type of flitch can always be found in a tree that has developed reaction wood. If it is reaction wood it will have some undesirable shrinkage characteristics (note chapter 7 on log defects).

The cracking in radial-cut flitches (figure 24, D) is greatly reduced because there is very little differential in length of annual rings *a* and *b*. In like manner, the plane-sawed flitch (figure 24, B) has a low differential between *a* and *b*.

Logs that contain a branch on one side should be sectioned in such manner to separate the dense wood of that branch for crotch grain (figure 25, A). The branch portion may be saved for hard carving but beautiful figure (figure 9, lower). If the branch is small, it may be cut as a radial flitch. It should be remembered that branch growth extends only from the pith upward and is not part of the structure on the opposite side of the tree. The flitch opposite the branch will be of straight grain.

Flitching of a large branch from a bolt prevents one from obtaining flitches of the largest size in wood of straight grain quality. This has led me to experimentation in bolts of three flitches. As in the other flitching process that I have used extensively the pitch is excluded; however, the "boxed heart" is triangular in shape (figure 25, A) instead of square (figure 23, I). It appears that this surface produced in the removal of the boxed heart is not as subject to cracking as that noted in the inner surface of the typical billet (note figure 42). Unfortunately I do not have a definitive answer to the comparative qualities of drying, checking, and cracking encountered in these two approaches. I am in the midst of experimentation with bolts of three flitches cut from different species and of different sizes. Experimentation never ends with organic material. It is not as predictable as steel or concrete. Join me in the search.

Under some circumstances flitches must be cut for discard. In the more northerly climates frost checks and regrowth can be seen on trees as a callous healing parallel to the trunk of the tree. A similar callous is formed following lightning strike of the tree. A narrow radial flitch includng either of this type of callous should be discarded (figure 25, B).

One small portion of the log, the inner heart, should not be saved. It is a small portion surrounding the pith (figure 26) with wide annual rings and weak wood. It is here that heart checks begin to develop under the slightest drying conditions. Although composed

A temperature-control paraffin pot and bench brush to clean surface prior to painting ends with paraffin.

The author's lode of flitches.

Torso from black walnut. Carved by author.

A

FIGURE 25. Flitching for crotch figure (A). The flitch cut for discard (B) may contain a frost check or a lightning scar. The callous healing parallel to the trunk of the tree appears the same for both.

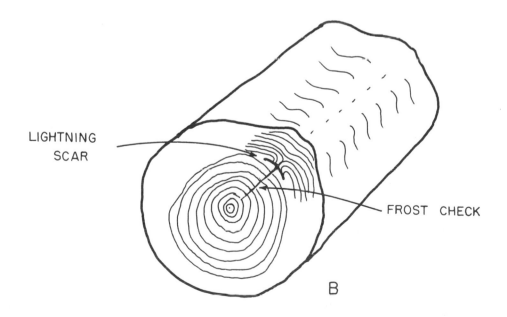

LIGHTNING SCAR

FROST CHECK

B

FIGURE 26. A basswood log with sufficient asymmetry for one large billet, a smaller second one to the right and two radial flitches. The small square enclosing the pith must be "boxed out."

of heartwood, it represents only a small portion of heartwood. "Box the heart" for discard.

The billets and flitches once well defined in the mind of the sawyer or marked on the log as in figure 23, 24, 25 and 26 can be cut in a line parallel to the growth form of the trunk. The chain saw was not designed to make this slablike cut. If the cut is made parallel to the pith, the chippers on the saw remove extremely long shavings that jam the mechanism, overwork the saw, and cause excessive heating (figure 27). The problem of jamming can be largely prevented if the cut is made at a slight angle to the pith. The chips that are cut break readily and are ejected as short pieces.

FIGURE 27. Sawing parallel to the pith causes binding of the saw with wood cuttings, which results in overheating of the bar and chain and unnecessary overloading of the entire tool.

Contrast of types of chips of these two angles of cut can be seen in figure 28.

During these first plane saw cuts, it is essential to have the log stabilized with wedges of wood to keep it from rolling and to permit maximum control with the saw (figure 26).

Two tangential cuts are made on the outside of the log if no wane edge is to be retained (figure 29). The wane edge (outer preimeter of sapwood) may be kept for carvings that require this extra portion of thickness. Two other cuts are made through the log, which include the pith and release a flitch of radial-sawed wood. Upon completion of these four cuts, one obtains three slabs of

FIGURE 28. Cutting at an angle to the pith yet in the same plane produces short chips, thereby reducing stress on chain saw. Note the two types of wood chips: long and undesirable cuttings to the left and short and desirable cuttings to the right.

wood (figure 30). The heart must then be boxed for discard in the middle or radial cut. Each section of the log is thus cut into its flitches (figure 31). The delightful lode of wood can now be taken home for further treatment and dreaming.

It is at this time that each billet and radial-sawed flitch or any other pieces ultimately to reach the carver's bench should be dated and weighed. The bathroom scales can also serve the wood weight watcher (note chapter 6 on drying the flitch). The species, the size of the flitch, and first date of weighing should be marked on each one immediately (figure 32). Use a broad, felt pen to record the above data on the rough wood surface.

FIGURE 29. Two tangential cuts that remove the wane edge and two radial cuts on either side of the pith.

FIGURE 30. Three basswood flitches. The radial flitch (center) is yet to have its heart boxed.

FIGURE 31. Flitches obtained from the 14-foot basswood log of figure 19.

FIGURE 32. Flitches of four hardwood species, labeled with size and weight at each month of weighing.

5

Preparation of the Flitch

Clear the decks, sweep the garage, prepare space for the new acquisition of flitches that have been cut in the woods. Too long a wait between the cutting of the flitch and sealing of its ends can destroy the flitch with checking and cracking. The following instructions prepare the flitch so as to reduce to a minimum the probability of checking and cracking. Since the structure of wood is made up of elongate cells aligned or arranged parallel to the pith, it is the excised cells that must be capped. Rate of water loss at the end of a flitch or log is 10 to 15 times as rapid as that water loss that passes in a perpendicular alignment from the pith. If the cells at the ends are exposed to drying, these cells are the first to dry and shrink. Stresses developed in this too-rapid drying at the ends of the flitch are followed by cell rupture, checking and cracking along the weak ray structures. If paraffin is applied properly at the ends of the flitch, the cells become impregnated and thus form a barrier against the loss of water.

The equipment needed for this operation can be developed from items in the home. The most important item is some type of temperature control unit which will contain paraffin or candle wax. A deep-fat fryer is excellent if temperatures below 212°F can be maintained. A double cooker does this inexpensively and it can be assembled from the kitchen without so much as a raised eyebrow from your spouse. A bench brush from the shop should be used to clean the surfaces prior to painting with hot paraffin. Any paintbrush will serve well to apply the hot paraffin (figure 33). It need not be cleaned from one paraffin application to the next. The paraffin can be purchased in pound blocks at the grocery store from the canning supplies section. This is paraffin used for sealing preserves

FIGURE 33. A temperature-control paraffin pot and bench brush to clean surface prior to painting ends with paraffin. The application should be done on a large sheet of plywood or hard fiberboard so waste wax can be recovered. The transparent cover of wax on the walnut log to the left assures no loss of moisture from the ends. The opaque application to the right is not a good seal. Checking and cracking will follow. On the wane (outer left) of the left-hand flitch can be seen the difference in color of the heartwood and the sapwood (the lighter-colored wood).

and jellies. I have found Gulfwax 33 manufactured by the Gulf Oil Company the best. It has a melting point of 133°F and spreads as lightly as water when heated to 170-180°F. It comes in 55-pound cases at almost one-third the cost of paraffin purchased at the grocery store. Candle wax can also be used; however, its higher melting point makes application difficult. The last item of equipment, a blowtorch or propane torch, will have special application as described in the latter part of this chapter.

The technique is as follows: Be sure the largest end of the flitch is squared. During the drying and storage period it will stand on end so that the air can circulate to all unparaffined surfaces. Brush both ends clean and apply hot paraffin in a thin and penetrating coat. Penetration of the paraffin is assured only if the surface is dry and warm. A test of the correct technique it to observe whether or not the applied paraffin is transparent, that is, the annual rings and the wood structure are readily observed through the coat. If, however, the application is opaque, one of two or both requirements have not been met (figure 33). If the surface is wet, paraffin cannot fill the excised cells. If the flitch is cold, the paraffin solidifies before filling the cells. An opaque layer is an indication that there is an air space between the paraffin and the wood structure. In time it will chip off, moisture will be lost too rapidly from the ends of the flitch, and checking will follow.

To avoid these errors, one may test the surface with the bare hand prior to application of the paraffin. Dampness can be readily detected, and if such a condition exists, the flitch should be permitted a period of drying just short of fine checking. On the other hand, if a cold surface exists, the flitch should be brought inside a warm room until its temperature adjusts to that of the surroundings. Large blocks that weigh 100 to 200 pounds not so easily moved can be treated with a blowtorch or propane torch. The surface is sprayed with the hot flame until it is dry and warm. Application of hot paraffiin is made immediately.

There will be times when the paraffin has been applied and an opaque cover is produced. Rather than saw a section of the flitch off or scrape the paraffin coat, I have used the blowtorch to melt the paraffin and heat the flitch simultaneously. One precaution, however, with this technique. Paraffin vaporized under high temperatures is highly inflammable. Do not quench the flame with water, smother with a wet cloth.

Never prepare hot paraffin directly over a flame or hot plate. As pointed out above, vaporized paraffin is highly inflammable. There is too much chance of forgetting a boiling pot of paraffin. It is for this reason that a temperature-controlled unit or a double boiler hot-water bath is preferred.

If the flitch has contained within its side surface the remnants of former limbs, that is, knots, hot paraffin should be applied to this end grain. If the flitch has been properly sealed on all end grain, moisture loss will be gradual (as noted in the following chapter).

The stresses developed throughout the drying process will be distributed over a long period of time and thus reduce to a minimum the probability of checking and cracking.

6

Drying the Flitch

Wood evolves as tissues for support of the tree and conductance of food and water. Wood was not conceived for the purpose of man. Primitive man has worked and the present-day wood technologist must work within the organic constraints of these tissues. To ignore this premise is to invite trouble.

Failure to flitch properly and to follow careful drying procedures lead to deformed creations (figure 34) and disappointment. Some sculptors take refuge in the thought that this is the "truth of the material." They have failed to recognize the organic constraints of wood, especially as expressed during the drying process. These tragedies can be minimized during the flitching and in using careful drying procedures.

The craftsman that works flitches directly from the tree recognizes differences between trees of the same species and differences within the same tree. The limb and trunk of the same tree cannot be expected to be of identical structure. Constraints increase with the size of the flitch, a principle that should be remembered. Each flitch, therefore, must be treated as unique. Wood is not a product of technology.

The thoughtful craftsman or wood-sculptor in extending the ideas above will utilize the strengths and weaknesses or imperfections in each bolt to his creative advantage. He cuts from the bolt flitches that will serve a patricular objective. These craftsmen are the applied wood technologists. They have been part of creative society since man first began using wood for his work and cultural pursuits.

The selection, cutting, and drying of bolts and flitches often are trade secrets of questionable integrity. Techniques of cutting and

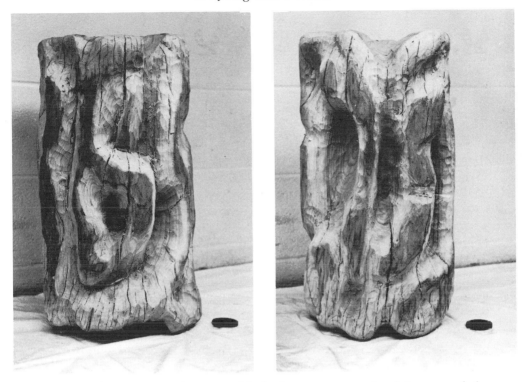

FIGURE 34. A wood sculpture in black cherry not completed because of the disappointment seen in severe checking and cracking.

drying that have been found worthwhile are seldom shared. Some based on "reason" are the right thing for the wrong reason. Some techniques are outright myth. I am reminded of Epictetus (first to second century A.D.) who observed that there were only four ways of making an observation: "Appearances to the mind are of four kinds. Things either are what they appear to be; or they neither are, nor appear to be; or they are, and do not appear to be; or they are not, and yet appear to be. Rightly to aim in all these cases is the wise man's task."

Much is known about air-drying standard lumber cuts as one- and two-inch dimensional stock (Rietz and Page, 1971). There is some difficulty in reconciling the problems and phenomena of air-drying lumber properly piled with the air-drying of flitches. The principles are the same, but the practices must of necessity be different. Flitches cannot be stacked. There appears to be no readily available data and methodology on the drying of large-dimensional

pieces. I have followed, over a period of three years, the change
in weight and condition of several species of flitches varying from
½ pound to well over 250 pounds. I shall share with you my reading, my experimentation, and practical experience in the drying
and carving of these. Hopefully I will neither develop nor per-
petuate any old wood-carver's tales nor contribute to an esoteric
and spurious technology. I shall try to follow the admonition of
Epictetus.

It is more meaningful to the practical craftsman or wood-carver
to first learn the simple procedures of determining change in the
weight of a flitch during the drying process before attempting to
learn the details of drying itself. If one wants to know how and
why drying takes place, he can pursue the latter portions of this
chapter.

At the outset, however, he should learn the first practical principles of drying a flitch for purposes of carving.

As an example of the drying process and the means of checking
the progress of drying I will use data from the flitches shown in
figure 32. These flitches represent three types of hardwood structures, considerable variation in flitch size, and time at which the

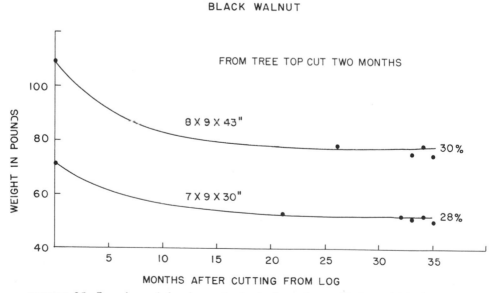

FIGURE 35. Loss in weight through air-drying of two flitches of black walnut
taken from treetop two months after tree was felled. The two flitches are
pictured in figure 32.

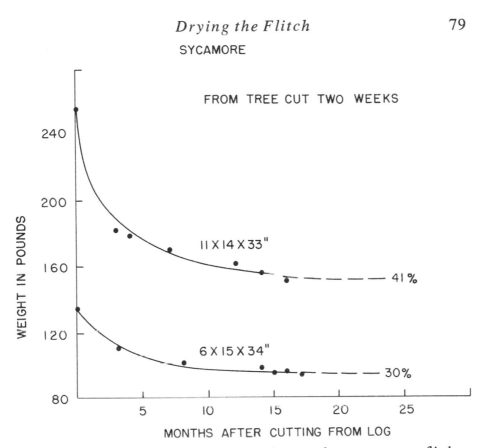

FIGURE 36. Loss in weight through air-drying of two sycamore flitches taken from tree that had been felled two weeks. The two flitches are pictured in figure 32.

flitch was cut with respect to the condition of the tree or log. Data for the change in weight have been plotted (figure 35 through 38).

Characteristically, all freshly cut flitches lose the major portion of their weight in a relatively short time. The rapidity with which this occurs among the four species is evident upon examining the above figures. Unfortunately, the time between the first and second measurement in weight change with the black walnut flitches covered a period of approximately two years. The slopes of the left-hand side of the curves, therefore, are only approximate. In the other three species, however, the immediate loss in weight is well defined, especially so in the sycamore and basswood (figures 36 and 38).

It is apparent that the black walnut flitches reached an equilibrium in weight toward the end of three years. The fluctuations indicated on the right-hand side of figure 35 are a reflection in low and high relative humidity for each of the last three months recorded. These two flitches, the small and large one, lost 28 and 30 percent respectively of their original weight.

Although the sycamore flitches lost a great portion of their original weight (figure 36), it appears from an extension of the curves that they will have reached equilibrium with the atmosphere in which they are stored in approximately two years. The larger flitch will have lost the larger portion of its weight (41 percent) and the smaller flitch will have lost 30 percent of its original weight in this period of time.

The black cherry flitch will have reached equilibrium also in approximately two years. At that time it will have lost approximately 20 percent of its original weight as determined from an extension of the curve from the left-hand to the right-hand side of figure 37. If this flitch had been cut from a living tree, a larger weight loss would have been noted. The 20 percent loss in weight is that ultimately to be experienced from this flitch cut from a dead standing tree.

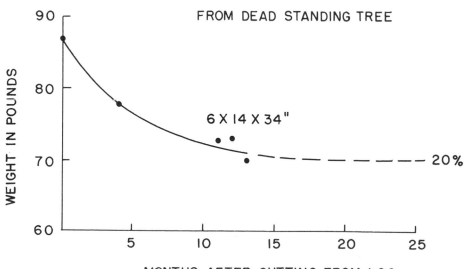

FIGURE 37. Loss in weight through air-drying of a flitch of black cherry taken from a dead, standing tree. The flitch is pictured in figure 32.

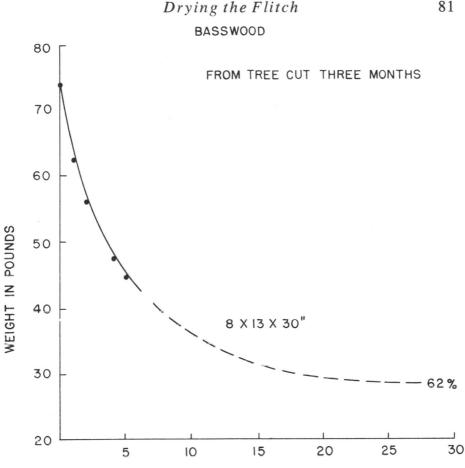

FIGURE 38. Loss in weight through air drying of a flitch of basswood taken from a tree that had been felled three months. The flitch is pictured in figure 32.

The basswood flitch, in the short period of five months, lost 32 percent of its original weight. At its indicated rate of change in weight, it should lose approximately 62 percent of its original weight in 30 months.

This technique of determining the time of equilibration in weight is relatively simple: weigh and plot change in weight with time. Certainly one need not weigh a flitch every month unless he is particularly interested in noting the initial rapid loss in weight, longer periods are required to obtain any changes in weight near the end of the drying process. The details of these dynamics will be discussed in the following part of this chapter.

The equilibrium weight of a flitch in terms of moisture content is called the equilibrium moisture content (EMC). The EMC of the flitches previously described reflect the effect of average long-term relative humidity and temperature conditions that exist in my garage. A covered shed would have provided conditions for the same EMC. If these flitches had been exposed to a higher relative humidity, their equilibrium weight would have been higher and the probability of checking further reduced. Likewise, if they had been brought into the home during the extreme dry conditions common to most homes in the winter, further loss in weight of each flitch would have been inevitable and accompanied with higher probability of checking and cracking. Atmospheric conditions of the home in winter are generally those for a lower EMC. It should be remembered, however, that the air-conditioned home in summer maintains humidity for an EMC near 5 percent. The air-conditioned home provides a southwestern desert condition without high temperature.

Thoroughly air-dried wood contains from 12 to 15 percent moisture content in the greater part of the United States. This is an equilibrium moisture content that reflects the average temperature and relative humidity obtained in sheltered but unheated areas. Of course, the potential equilibrium moisture content differs in summer and winter, because temperature and relative humidity conditions of the atmosphere differ in these two periods (table 7). The potential EMC is higher during the winter in all general regions of the United States. The overall highest moisture conditions exist in the New England states, the northcentral United States, and central and eastern Canada. Areas closely associated with large bodies of water have their own unique atmospheric conditions. The data of table 7 are not applicable to local areas of each region. The driest climate conditions occur throughout the southwestern United States where both the July and January potential EMC of 7 to 8 percent are those of modern kiln drying. These relative humidity conditions are somewhat comparable to many heated homes of the North in the wintertime and air-conditioned homes in the summer.

Lumber used in furniture must be kiln dried to near 5 percent. High temperatures and low humidities are employed to establish a gradient from the outside to the inside of lumber so that moisture will move in that gradient to evaporation. Removal of additional water from thoroughly air-dried wood requires an exposure to lower humidity.

TABLE 7

RELATIONSHIP OF AVERAGE RELATIVE HUMITY AT NOON FOR VARIOUS AREAS OF THE
UNITED STATES AND CANADA AND THE EQUILIBRIUM MOISTURE CONTENT[a]

REGION	SEASON	AVERAGE RELATIVE HUMIDTY	AVERAGE DRY BULB TEMPERATURE °F	EQUILIBRIUM MOISTURE CONTENT
New England	July	60-70	65-70	12
States	January	70-80	15-30	15
Southeastern	July	50-65	70-90	10
United States	January	60-70	30-50	12
Northcentral	July	45-65	65-70	10
United States	January	70-85	5-15	16
Mid-central	July	40-55	70-80	9
United States	January	60-70	20-40	12
Southcentral	July	50-65	80	10
United States	January	60 70	40 50	12
Northwest	July	25-40	60-70	7
United States	January	60-80	20-30	13
Southwestern	July	30-35	70-90	7
United States	January	35-45	30-50	8
Western Canada	July	35-60	60-70	9
	January	75-85	20-30	16
Central Canada	July	45-65	60-65	10
	January	75-85	—5-10	16
Eastern Canada	July	60-70	60-70	12
	January	70-80	5-20	15

[a] Adapted from Climate and Man. *1941 Yearbook of Agriculture,* U. S. Department of
Agriculure, and Rietz and Page, 1971.

If one wishes to make certain of the moisture content in a flitch,
he can do so by application of an electronic moisture tester (figure
39). Application to the plane- or radial sawed wood will give a
measure representative of conditions on the interior. The higher the
quantity of moisture left in the flitch, the greater the conduction of
electricity between the two electrodes. This conduction of current is
translated to percent moisture content. If the moisture content as
measured with the moisture meter is significantly above the EMC
for the particular area in which you live, obviously there is moisture
yet to be lost from the flitch.

The wood technologist measures moisture content of lumber on
the greater width dimension, the face of the board, in the manner
as pictured (figure 39). The electrodes have been designed to
measure moisture content from the surface to approximately 1.5
inches depth. They must be placed parallel to the grain as shown

FIGURE 39. Use of a moisture tester to measure moisture content of a flitch. The electrodes must be placed in the wood parallel with the grain.

so as to minimize the electrical resistance from cell walls. Placed across the grain they would encounter greater resistance and thus give a false low reading.

Not having a moisture meter, one may approach the calculation of moisture content in the flitch by comparing the weight of that particular species and volume of flitch with what it would be at oven-dry conditions. Oven-dry weight is the weight of a cubic foot of wood when all bound water is lost. It is obtained by maintaining wood at 212°F (100°C) until there is no further change in the weight of the wood. The specific gravity is based upon the oven-dry weight and is compared to water, which has a specific gravity of 1.0. Water weighs 62.4 pounds per cubic foot, therefore, a cubic foot of wood with a specific gravity of .50 would weigh 31.2 pounds per cubic foot. If one takes the total volume of any flitch that appears to have reached its equilibrium moisture content (there is no longer a weight loss with time) and equates this volume to the weight of a cubic foot of the same wood oven dried (table 8), he *can* employ the following formula to obtain its moisture content:

$$\text{moisture content} = \frac{\begin{array}{c}\text{weight of wood} \\ \text{and moisture}\end{array} - \begin{array}{c}\text{oven dry weight} \\ \text{of wood}\end{array}}{\text{oven dry weight of wood}} \times 100$$

Most likely when these calculations are made, it will be found that the moisture content is slightly above the EMC expected. This last loss of weight in moisture is a very slow process (refer again to figure 35 through 38). It can be hastened by exposing the flitch to lower humidity. This increase is gradient of humidity from the interior to the outside will cause moisture to move from the flitch to the outside.

TABLE 8

REPRESENTATIVE WOODS OF NORTH AMERICA: THEIR SPECIFIC GRAVITY AND WOOD SHRINKAGE IN % OF GREEN VOLUME FROM GREEN TO OVEN DRY CONDITION[a]

SPECIES	SPECIFIC GRAVITY	WOOD SHRINKAGE			RATIO: $\frac{T}{R}$	EASE OF CARVING
		VOLUME	RADIAL	TANGENTIAL		
Alder, red	.45	12.6	4.4	7.3	1.61	A
Ash, white	.66	12.6	4.2	6.5	1.55	C
Aspen, quaking	.38	11.1	3.3	6.9	2.09	B
Bald cypress	.51	10.7	3.8	6.0	1.58	B
Basswood	.32	15.8	6.6	9.3	1.41	A
Beech	.56	16.2	4.8	10.6	2.21	C
Birch, yellow	.55	16.8	7.4	9.0	1.22	C
Buckeye, yellow	.40	12.0	3.5	7.8	2.23	B
Butternut	.36	10.2	3.3	6.1	1.85	A
Caltalpa	.47	7.3	—	—	—	A
Cedar, Atlantic white	.35	—	2.9	5.4	1.86	A
Cedar, eastern red	.44	7.8	3.1	4.7	1.51	A
Cedar, incense	.35	7.6	3.3	5.7	1.73	A
Cedar, Port Orford	.40	10.7	5.2	8.1	1.56	A
Cedar, western red	.31	8.1	2.5	5.1	2.04	A
Cherry, black	.47	11.5	3.7	7.1	1.92	C
Cottonwood, eastern	.45	14.1	3.9	9.2	2.36	B
Dogwood, flowering	.81	19.9	7.1	11.3	1.59	C
Elm, American	.46	14.4	4.2	9.5	2.26	C
Fir, Douglas Pacific Coast	.45	12.6	5.0	7.9	1.58	C
Fir, balsam	.34	10.8	2.8	6.6	2.36	B
Fir, grand	.35	10.6	3.2	7.2	2.25	B
Fir, white	.42	10.2	3.4	7.0	2.06	B

TABLE 8

REPRESENTATIVE WOODS OF NORTH AMERICA: THEIR SPECIFIC GRAVITY AND WOOD
SHRINKAGE IN % OF GREEN VOLUME FROM GREEN TO OVEN DRY CONDITION[a]

| SPECIES | SPECIFIC GRAVITY | WOOD SHRINKAGE | | | RATIO: $\frac{T}{R}$ | EASE OF CARVING |
		VOLUME	RADIAL	TANGENTIAL		
Gum, black tupelo	.46	12.5	4.2	7.6	1.81	C
Gum, sweet	.54	—	5.3	10.2	1.92	C
Hemlock, eastern	.38	10.4	3.0	6.4	2.13	B
Hickory, shagbark	.64	16.7	7.0	10.5	1.50	C
Holly	.64	16.2	4.5	9.5	2.11	B
Laurel, California (Oregon myrtle)	.62	11.6	—	—	—	A
Locust, black	.48*	9.8	4.4	6.9	1.57	C
Madrone, Pacific	.74	17.3	—	—	—	C
Maple, Oregon or Bigleaf	.54	11.6	3.7	7.1	1.92	C
Maple, sugar	.56	14.5	4.8	9.2	1.92	C
Oak, California black	.64	12.1	3.6	6.6	1.83	C
Oak, red	.56	14.2	3.9	8.3	2.13	C
Oak, laurel	.71	19.0	3.9	9.5	2.44	C
Osage, orange	.85	8.9	—	—	—	C
Pecan	.60	16.0	4.9	8.9	1.82	B
Pine, lodgepole	.38	11.5	4.5	6.7	1.49	B
Pine, longleaf	.54	12.3	5.3	7.5	1.42	C
Pine, Norway (red)	.41	11.5	4.6	7.2	1.57	B
Pine, sugar	.35	8.4	2.9	5.6	1.93	A
Pine, eastern white	.34	7.8	2.2	5.9	2.68	A
Pine, western yellow (ponderosa)	.38	10.0	3.9	6.4	1.64	A
Poplar, yellow	.38*	11.4	4.1	6.9	1.68	A
Redwood	.38	6.3	2.7	4.2	1.55	B
Sassafras	.51	10.3	4.0	6.2	1.55	B
Spruce, sitka	.37	11.2	4.5	7.4	1.64	B
Spruce, white	.37	14.8	3.7	7.3	1.97	B
Sycamore	.46	14.2	5.1	7.6	1.49	C
Walnut, black	.51	11.3	5.2	7.1	1.37	B
Willow, black	.34	13.8	2.6	7.8	3.00	B

SOURCE: Adapted from Koehler, 1924; Rich, 1970; Forest Products Laboratory, 1935; Rietz and Page, 1971; and U. S. Department of Agriculture, 1949.

[a] Shrinkage is based upon green to oven dry condition. However, wood is not commerically treated to oven dry condition but is kiln dried or air dried, therefore, about ½ to ⅔ as much of the shrinkage indicated need be expected.

[b] Based on weight when oven dry calculated with green volume.

[c] A, relatively high workability, B, intermediate and C is relatively low.

*At 12% moisture content.

Wood is a hygroscopic substance. When the humidity is high it takes up water. When the humidity is low it loses water. In a sense it can be likened unto a sponge. Wood does not breath, wood does not season, not in the time periods considered by the woodcarver. Wood in a violin that has been played for many years does "season". It changes somehow to produce a more vibrant resonance than freshly prepared wood. Also, as wood ages it changes in color. White pine turns yellow. Some woods turn to a deep red, a pink, or a grey (table 9). Our primary concern, however, is that wood gives up moisture or takes on moisture depending upon the relationship of atmospheric humidity and the moisture content of the flitch at any particular time.

TABLE 9

CHANGES IN THE COLOR OF WOOD EXPOSED TO THE ATMOSPHERE

White pine: white	yellow
Osage orange: yellow	deep red
Black cherry: light tan	brown
Elm: yellow	brown
Beech: yellow	red or pink
Sycamore: pink	yellow
Walnut: chocolate brown	grey
Redwood: red brown	grey

The more open the cellular structure, the greater the loss of weight from green condition to oven-dry or EMC condition. The denser the cellular structure, the less the loss. Compare the flitches as described in figure 35 and 38 (black walnut versus basswood). Basswood is an open cellular structure whereas black walnut is much denser.

If wood were truly solid, that is, if there were no cellular spaces, the specific gravity would be 1.46. One cubic foot would weigh 91 pounds. There would be no moisture content, for there would be no space for moisture in such a cube. The density of various species of wood, therefore, is a function of the cellular space to total volume. Basswood as noted in table 8 has a specific gravity of 0.32, whereas, osage orange and flowering dogwood have a specific gravity of 0.81. Therefore, there is greater capacity for moisture in basswood and this is indicated by its rapid loss in weight (figure 38). In genreal, this relationship between specific gravity and capacity to hold water varies from zero at a specific gravity of 1.46 to 200 percent at a specific gravity of 0.37 (table 10). Basswood of low specific gravity therefore undergoes a large weight loss from green to any EMC or oven-dry condition.

TABLE 10

The General Relationship of Capacity[a] to Hold Water and the Specific Gravity of Woods at Oven-Dry Condition

Specific Gravity	% of Water[b]
0.37	200
0.45	150
0.60	100
0.88	50
1.46	0

[a] Adapted from Koehler, 1924.

[b] Weight of water that can be contained based upon oven-dry weight.

$$M = \frac{1.46\text{-}S}{S \times 1.46} \times 100 \text{ when}$$

$$M = \% \text{ water; } S = \text{specific gravity}$$

As mentioned earlier, wood is a hygroscopic material. It has sorptive cell surface, i.e., cell walls that take up or give up water. Sorptive surfaces and water-holding capacity are inversely related to the specific gravity of wood (note table 10). The total area exposed to water absorption, that is, water uptake (absorption) or water release (desorption), is large. There are three types of surface. A one-inch cube block of wood of specific gravity 0.42 (redwood and eastern hemlock both with specific gravity of 0.38 near this value) has a total external area of 6 square inches, the first and obvious type of surface. The area of exposed cell cavities on those six surfaces covers approximately 15 square feet, the second type of surface. The surface area of fibrils (300,000,000 on the surface area (the third type of surface) of approximately 22,000 square feet (Brown, Panskin, and Forsaith, 1952). Such a surface provides wood the structure for rapid gain or loss of moisture with short but marked changes in relative humidity. This can be seen in figures 35, 36, and 37 in the next-to-last period of weighing, a month of intense rainfall related to the great floods of Hurricane Agnes in the northeastern United States during June 1972.

Change in weight, however, due to changes in relative humidity once the EMC is reached, is relatively small. The larger changes in weight occur immediately after cutting a flitch from a downed tree. The cells are fiilled with free water called unbound water, a large part of the weight of a "green" log. Therefore, it is easily lost through vessels of hardwoods and trachieds of the conifers. If the ends of the flitches are sealed, then water loss occurs through the cell walls and through the ray structures of parenchyma tissue. There is no shrinkage of the cellular structure in this type of drying.

The initial loss of unbound water would be much more rapid if the ends of the flitch were not sealed with paraffin. Water loss through the ends of an unsealed flitch is about 15 times as rapid as through the lateral walls of the cells and ray parenchyma.

Once all the free water has been evaporated from a flitch, it is at the fiber saturation point (FSP), a moisture content of from 25 to 35 percent for most woods. Below the FSP cell walls begin to shrink as their moisture content comes in balance with the atmospheric conditions. This loss of water is bound water, that is water molecules that are chemically bound within the cell walls. The energy required to drive this moisture out is much higher than for loss under the unbound moisture condition. More energy is required per unit loss in moisture as the water content is decreased. Kiln-drying with its high heat, low humidity, and exhaust-fan operation provides these conditions. Without this short-term input of energy, air-drying must of necessity be slower. That portion of the curve which is almost flat (figure 35 through 38) is the period in which further water loss well below the fiber saturation point is very slow. Therefore, much more time is required per unit loss of weight in air-drying than in kiln-drying.

As mentioned previously, the moisture content equilibrates with the temperature and humidity conditions averaged in the particular area of storage. This is known as the equilibrium moisture content and can be calculated for any given measure of relative humidity and temperature or wet-bulb temperature (figure 40). Let us look at this figure more carefully and consider what conditions exist for thoroughly air-dried wood at 12 to 15 percent moisture content, conditions for air-drying wood in the greater part of the United States. The EMC of 12 to 15 percent would occur in a relative humidity range of approximately 70 percent over a range of temperatures of 0° to approximately 60° F. The wet-bulb depression over this range could range from approximately 2° to 8°F.

Contrast these outside drying conditions with those occuring in most homes in the northern part of the United States during the depth of winter. In many homes, temperatures may range from 70° to 75°F with relative humidity generally under 20 percent and wet-bulb depression, as much as 23 to 27°F. Checking these values on figure 40 one can see the equilibrium moisture content for wood in a home would be approximately 2 percent. These are kiln-drying conditions. Moisture loss of bound water is relatively rapid accompanied with shifts in stress in the cellular strutcure. Considerable energy is used in heating the cold, dry winter air to summerlike temperatures. The high relative humidity of cold air is lowered

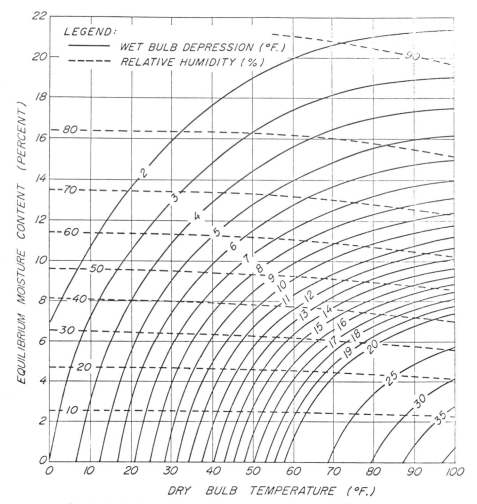

FIGURE 40. Relative humidity of the air and the equilibrium moisture content of wood as related to the dry-bulb temperature and the wet-bulb depression. (From Rietz and Page, 1971, with permission of Forests Products Laboratory, Madison, Wisconsin)

appreciably when heated in the home. Such a change is reflected in the wet-bulb depression. Checking is imminent at this time. All flitches should be exposed gradually to this drastic change in humidity so as to permit time for redistribution of stresses.

A persistent old woodcraftsman tale is that air-drying of wood is best accomplished in the attic, but the principle of maintaining a gentle gradient of humidity from inside the flitch to the surrounding air is seldom obtained there. Humidity in most attics is extremely low in summer and high in winter. Cracking, wraping, and deformation are maximized. The attic should not be used for drying wood. Choose an area and structure that avoids extremes of humidity and preferably one that permits the maintenance of a controlled small negative atmospheric humidity (note chapter 8 on storage of wood.

One of the objectives that has been emphasized throughout this book has been the avoidance of any procedures that would tend toward the development of checks in the flitch. The importance and the techniques of hot paraffin application on the ends of the flitch have been shown as a means of reducing rapid moisture loss with accompanying checking. In the chapter on cutting of the flitch, there was brief consideration given to orientation of the cut with respect to the annular ring configuration. An understand of the dynamics of plant growth, cellular arrangement, cell wall shrinking, and stresses that are developed during the drying process should help the reader to avoid those circumstances that enhance checking and crack development in the flitch.

Basic to the following material should be an understanding of cell structure. The variation in cell wall thickness, size of cell itself, tensile and compression strengths, varies little within each type of wood structure within the flitch. Earlier it was pointed out that the area immediately around the pith should be "boxed out" so as to avoid the heart checking that develops readily in this wood.

Heartwood has extractives in the cells (not the cell walls); therefore is bulked. Shrinkage is hindered. In sapwood there are no extractives; therefore these cells are not bulked. Shrinkage occurs under slight drying, and rupture and checking ensue. Walls of sapwood and heartwood have the same thickness. Bulking makes the difference. It was suggested earlier that the bark could be left on the flitch to reduce the rate of drying and therefore to allow time for adjustment of stresses. These procedures protect the sapwood to some degree and reduce to a minimum cracking and checking in that area.

Simple as it may be, we need to keep in mind that the tree is simply an accretion of cones or layers upon layers of wood from one year to the next (figure 41, A). If the tree then is an accretion of cones of cellular material and the cells are all the same size in a particular type of wood, then as the tree grows a larger number of cells must be developed by the cambium to extend the circumference of the tree as it grows. The number of cells within the inner annual rings are smaller in number than those cells in later annual rings (figure 41, B). Once an individual cell matures at the growing tip or the outer edge of the cambium, it becomes filled with sap, contributes to the growth of the tree, and dies when it is transformed from sapwood to heartwood. The cell does not change its shape after its short period of maturation, but remains filled with liquid until it is processed for drying.

The differentiation or orientation of microfibrils in four layers of differing thickness is the cell wall, the degree of extractive deposits in the cells and the ratio of cell diameter to length coupled with differences in thickness of end cell walls and longitudinal cell walls cause differences in shrinkage along three major directional axes. All wood is characterized in these features as being anisotropic. As each cell loses part of its bound water, shrinkage follows in all dimensions of the cell.

Shrinkage of the cell occurs along its longitudinal axis (U-V of of figure 41, C) and along the diameter of its axis as radial shrinkage (W-X of figure 41, C) and tangential shrinkage (Y-Z of figure 41, C). Longitudinal shrinkage, that is shrinkage along the greater dimension of the cell which is aligned parallel to the pith, is minimal. Greater shrinkage occurs in the two planes, W-X shrinkage and Y-Z with this later shrinkage, tangential shrinkage, the greatest (table 8). The values given for tangential shrinkage are meaningful to those working in the production of lumber, and can be used by the wood-carver as an index of what to expect in potential cracking or splitting in a particular species. The ratio T/R (table 8) is an index to the problem of drying a flitch. The higher the ratio and the larger the cross-sectional dimension of the flitch, the greater the probability for the development of cracks. Furthermore, woods of high specific gravity with a high T/R ratio are those most difficult to dry without checking.

The combined radial shrinkage and tangential shrinkage act to reduce the diameter of a log and this reduction in circumference along each annual ring during drying results in the development of large cracks. The inner annuli have a sum of shrinkage within their cells that is much smaller than that occuring in the outer rings. This in effect produces a V-shape crack if all the shrinkage is summed in one portion of the log (figure 41, D). With this type of crack developing, obviously all the tension developed during the drying process is released in the one large crack. Of course, the larger the log the more inevitable is the development of a crack. Small logs can undergo drying without cracking, but these are generally of sizes less than five or six inches in diameter, a size not readily

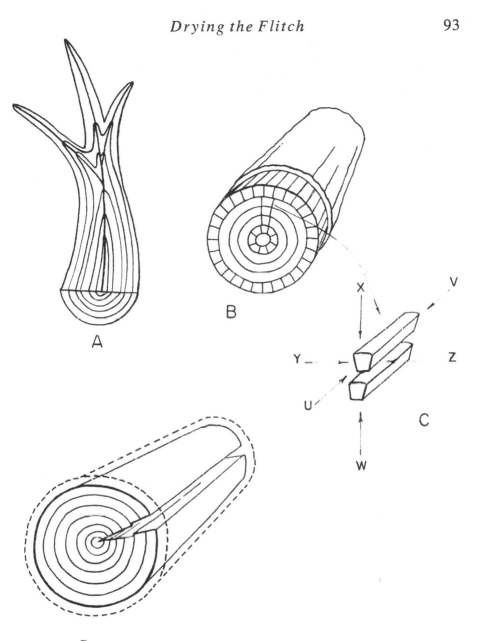

FIGURE 41. The diagramatic relationships of tree growth, cell shrinkage, and cracking in a log. The tree grows with the addition of a cylinder of cells for each year (A). The inner annuli have fewer cells than the outer annuli (B). Shrinkage of the cell (C) are of three general types: radial (W-X), tangential (Y-Z) and longitudinal (U-V). Tangential and radial shrinkage of cells are most obviously expressed in logs as circumferential shrinkage with ensuing cracking along the rays. Note expression of this shrinkage in carving of black cherry log (figure 34).

suitable for large carvings. Flitches, therefore, should be cut in such a manner to permit the release of this buildup of tension.

As you may recall, the bolt was cut into four flitches (figure 23). These four flitches undergo a drying process that results in little distortion and checking or splitting in the radial flitches but considerable distortion in the two large billets. Tension accumulated during the drying develops cracks along the ray parenchyma on the wain edge (sapwood) and on the side of the excluded pith (figure 42). Because of the tension developed circumferentially (the resultant of forces of differences in radial and tangential shrinkage along each annulus), there is a distortion of the billet as indicated by the dotted lines of figure 43.

The reduction in the width of the billet is traditionally described as tangential shrinkage, but the distortion of warping of the billet may also be described as a summation of differences in tangential and radial shrinkage along each annulus, a circumferential phenomenon. It is the resultant of differences in shrinkage of the short inner annuli versus those of the longer outer annuli that result in

FIGURE 42. Development of pith-side check in a large-dimension billet of walnut. The small checks occured as end checking following removal of the paraffin in preparation of the photograph.

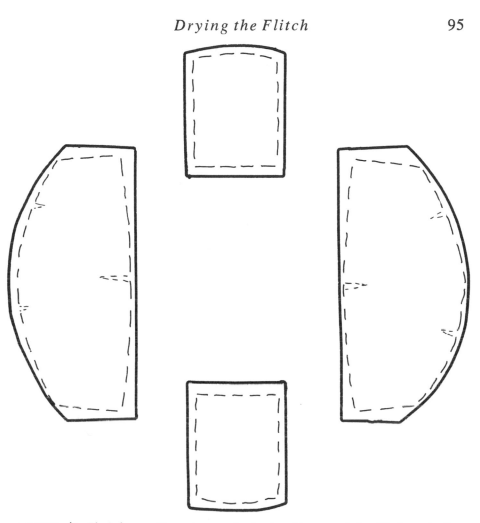

FIGURE 43. Shrinkage distortion and checks diagramed in flitches similar to that cut in figure 23. Solid outer lines mark the shape of flitches at the time of cutting; dotted lines mark the change in shape and shrinkage in drying.

the distortion and leads to cracking on the pith side. Radial flitches of the same size as the above billet would not be subject to such cracking, although the T/R values are the same. The difference is primarily one of differences in length of annual rings. Under section on cutting the flitch, these differences in annuli length are described as being important in selecting the planes in which the log should be cut. Application of these ideas to the actual carving are discussed further in chapter 9, Carving the Flitch.

It has been mentioned previously that there are no two trees of the same species alike, and wood from different parts of the same tree differs somewhat in structure. As one works with flitches from the same tree (figure 31) he soon learns of these differences. Some species are decidedly more difficult to work than others. Perhaps this is the wonderfully unpredictable (in absolute engineering terms) nature of things organic.

The craftsman must first understand the broad generalities and principles of the expression of stress in drying wood. He must note the apparent exceptions and look for logical explanations. With understanding of the general principles and experience in the apparent exceptions—all of which take time—and the application of awareness and curiosity, the craftsman arrives at a level of understanding wood that is part of the new creativity. He reduces his problems of cracking to a minimum by employing all the techniques of cutting and treatment at his disposal. He recognizes those flitches most subject to cracking and warping through their type of wood structure (burls, crotches, reaction wood, etc.). The more complex the irregularities of growth, the less predictable will be his avoidance of problems. This is not unique to us nor is it unique to the experienced kiln operator.

Most of the time we can predict what will happen to a flitch. If the structure is too complex for analysis then let it dry as it will. Use that which has dried to those levels for use. Observe and try to learn from each flitch. You will never learn it all, but you will greatly reduce your margin of error.

7

Log Defects

To the uninitiated, the exterior of a tree trunk or log tells nothing about the quality of the interior wood. Interior rot or abnormal growth remains an unknown until the novice applies ax or chain saw in the cutting of flitches. This should not be, however.

Just as the sculptor learns to see the details he wishes to carve, so should the seeker of wood picture what lies beneath the bark through an examination of the exterior bark. Bark is the revealer of much of the past history of the log. Just as wood cells are laid down to the inside and phloem to the outside by the cambium during each year of growth, so are cork cells laid down toward the bark side by the cork cambium. Unlike wood cells, the cork cells are eventually sloughed off the outer perimeter, however, they persist for a sufficiently long time to provide clues about the inner conditions of wood structure. Any mature tree of a given species has a pattern and texture of bark that is very uniform. Once the eye recognizes this uniformity, irregularities in the pattern or texture are readily discernible. These irregularities are cellular expressions of changes in the growth patterns of the past. Branches or knots that have become overgrown with tissue are covered with the most obvious bark pattern to that which is very subtle (figure 44). The latter, of course, contain only remnants of the past cellular change in cork growth.

Checks caused by exteremely low temperature conditions of winter (frost-check or lightening) are readily seen as an elongate scar of callous or deformed bark tissue (figure 25). Evidence of these damages to the tree remain apparent for many years beyond that noted for knots.

If the tree has been attacked by insects that destroy the cambium,

FIGURE 44. Obvious (*upper*) and subtle (*lower*) bark patterns that provide clues to the presence of knots and former limbs in the main trunk of the tree. The remnant of a former limb is much closer the surface in the tree trunk of the upper photograph.

loose bark accompanied with a depression in the general area of attack can readily be noticed. Some digging or prying will reveal the wood tissue. At the edges will be seen the development of new cambium and covering scar tissue.

The most obvious disruption in bark growth is seen where nails, wire, or other metallic materials become embedded in the tree growth (figure 16). Once wire or nails become enveloped or covered with cambial tissue, a protuberance or bump forms above or outside the area (figure 45) of its presence. An ax is the most effective and least expensive way of exploring the possibilities of this type of evidence.

Another type of log defect previously referred to as reaction wood should be avoided or if used shaped with the knowledge that splitting and cracking are highly probable. Reaction wood is of two types (tension and compression) and is developed quite distinctly in hardwoods and conifers respectively. Reaction wood develops in both these types of trees when the tree becomes displaced from its normal vertical position. It must realign its growth to establish a new center of gravity. In hardwoods there is an increase in the width of annual ring growth on the side of tree displacement

FIGURE 45. Protuberance of wood growth in yellow birch as indicative of an embedded nail, accompanied with evidence of wood stain above and below the nail.

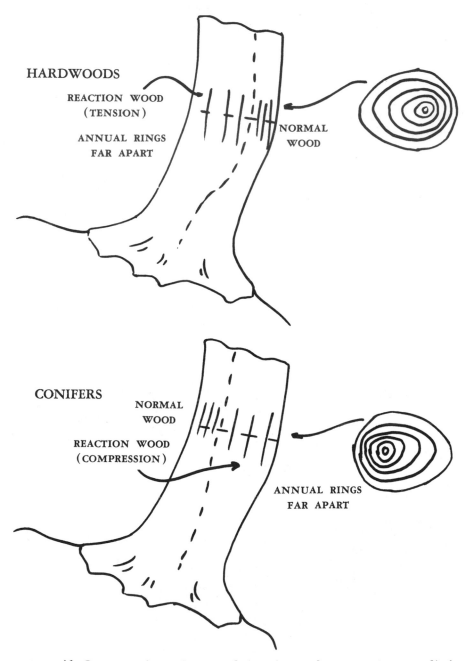

FIGURE 46. Contrast of reaction wood (tension and compression wood) in hardwoods and conifers respectively.

(figure 46). The reaction wood developed in hardwoods is known as tension wood because the treetop is, in effect, pulling against that portion of the tree trunk which is being enlarged in its development.

Conifers, on the other hand, displaced in the same manner, develop a reaction wood termed compression wood. This area of specialized cell structure is developed on that side of the tree to which displacement has occurred. The weight of the displaced treetop tends to compress cellular structure in this portion of the trunk.

Wood flitches cut from reaction wood of hardwoods tend to shrink abnormally in the longitudinal dimension. Furthermore, the cellular structure is of much greater density than that in other parts of the tree. It has more lignin and less cellulose than normal wood. Control of cracking is difficult and the wood is hard to work.

Compression wood formed in conifers on the underside of the bow has a longitudinal shrinkage often ten times that of normal wood. Tension wood in hardwoods that forms on the upper side of the bow has an abnormal longitudinal shrinkage, however, it is not as great as that in compression wood. The wood remains difficult to work.

Plant physiologists have determined that reaction wood develops as a result of the tree's hormonal structures sending auxins to that portion of the tree where such development needs to take place. It has not been determined, however, why hardwoods and conifers differ so diametrically in the location of reaction wood.

Internal rot is a defect that should be recognized before the tree is felled. It is generally initiated by the exposure of wood within the cambium to atmospheric conditions. This may be either in the form of a broken branch, a bruised limb, or a burned or scared root base of the tree. Any tree containing evidence of such nature should be suspect and may be examined for its soundness with an increment bore or brace and bit. The timbre of the tree trunk when struck with a hard object should tell something of the internal firmness of cell structure. The extent to which the above types of damage can cause decay and penetrate all tissues of that layer is well illustrated in the color figures of Shigo and Larsen (1969).

Learn to "read" the bark for its hidden irregularities. Note the uniform structure and texture of bark on trees that are well developed and well protected from all types of injury. Couple this with the reading of Brough (1969), Shigo and Larsen (1969), and Werner *et al.* (1964). The bark, although cryptic, is not inscrutable for the quality of wood beneath its fissured structure.

8

Storage of Wood

Aspects most closely related to the proper drying of wood relate primarily to the atmospheric conditions of the place of storage. Sudden changes in any environmental extreme should be avoided. Flitches should be stored where circulation of air is assured, where direct sunlight is avoided, and where moisture in the form of snow or rain cannot be driven into the place of storage.

As the flitch dries, there should exist an air moisture content only slightly below that of the wood. Under these conditions of humidity, no sudden stress is developed in the flitch. The cellular structure has an opportunity to give gradually to this change with minimal chance for cracking. Basements may on occasion be ideal; however, some offer ideal conditions for the development of fungi that stain or decay wood. Furthermore, air circulation is often hampered in these confined spaces. Under some circumstances, however, after a flitch has undergone its initial surface drying and particularly if it is a large flitch, the basement may offer a longer period for water loss and gradual adjustment of tension within the flitch than can be found in other storage areas. Those using a basement for this purpose need only keep an eye open for the development of fungi (discussion follows in the next section).

Most wood scavengers will find any outside storage or covered shed protected from rain as suitable. Racks can be constructed with two-by-fours as vertical standards and shelving made of two-by-eights or two-by-sixes in inexpensive softwoods. The only precaution to be applied in this type of storage is that those flitches placed close to the ceiling should be near the equilibrium moisture content (EMC) for the climate common to the particular section of the country. Flitches that are near or above the fiber saturation point should not be located near the upper shelves, since drying will proceed too rapidly. Case hardening develops when the outer surfaces of large flitches reach EMC in a short time.

Case hardening occurs when the cells in the outer portions of the flitch dry rapidly and well below the fiber saturation point. Shrinkage of the outer cells is restrained by the central portion of the flitch which is still above the fiber saturation point. A tension develops in the outer areas and compression develops within the flitch. Later when the flitch becomes uniformly dry the stresses are reversed. The outer layers undergo compression and the inner cells are in tension. Case hardening is a very common problem in the drying of large flitches. It can be reduced to a minimum through gradual drying so that there is a gentle gradient in equilibrium moisture content from the center of the flitch to near its surface. In addition to the physical problems of wood storage and drying are those biological in nature: fungi and insects.

Fungi of wood occur as primarily two types. There are many wood rotting fungi known as Basidiomycetes and molds which form dark stains in wood belong to the group of fungi known as Ascomycetes. Fungal growth is encouraged where there is humid conditions provided with oxygen and relatively high temperatures.

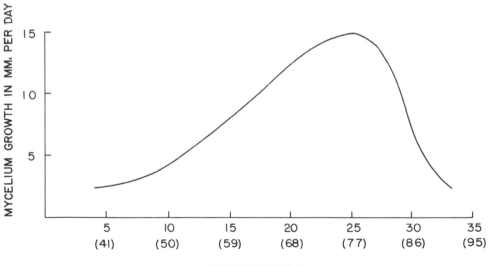

FIGURE 47. A general growth curve for fungi as related to temperature when oxygen and moisture conditions are optimal. Values in ( ) are degrees fahrenheit.

Spores of fungi are airborne and therefore can be expected to be found most everywhere. When the spores are blown or settle on wood with a high moisture content of 35 to 50 percent coupled with temperatures above or near 77° (25°C, note figure 47) growth proceeds vigorously. The living tree has too much water in its sapwood to permit the growth of fungi. And growth is difficult when the moisture is well below 20 percent.

Since fungi are aerobic, that is, they require oxygen, sawyers often keep logs in what is known as a "hot" pond in the winter or they maintain recently cut wood in summer under a continuous spray of water. The wood-carver is not likely to carry out this practice. He must surface dry the wood quickly to check fungal growth.

When the spores germinate under warm humid conditions, an hyphal thread grows to form a meshwork of hyphae known as mycelium. The growth of mycelium penetrates the tissues under optimum moisture and temperature conditions. Growth of some species continues under temperatures as high as 110°F (43°C), but most often the growth is markedly reduced near 100°F (38°C). Growth is stopped with below-freezing temperatures but growth is resumed as soon as temperatures return to summertime conditions. From freezing temperatures to the optimum growing temperatures, a 20° increase in temperature doubles the rate of fungal growth. From 40 to 60 degrees there is a doubling in growth; from 40 to 80 degrees rate of growth is quadrupled. This is reason enough for not leaving logs on the ground during the summer. Fungi invade rapidly and destroy very quickly the quality of wood in a log.

Killing fungi by heating is not practical in the home. It can be done, however, in a dry kiln with high temperature and steam-heat conditions. One to two hours are needed at 150°F. This temperature, to be effective, must reach the innermost cellular structure of the flitch. Charring the surface, a practice that has been used in the past, does not kill the deep-seated mycelium. Chemical sprays are of little utility on flitches that contain the mycelium fungi, since the fungi penetrate the inner cells. It cannot be expected that any type of poison spray would reach these growth structures of the fungi.

Fungi within the wood causes a change in color and weakens the cellular structure. It often prepares the wood for insect attack and it changes the fragrance of wood to that of a mushroom odor. The discoloration with northern hardwood trees is beautifully illustrated in color by the work previously noted of Shigo and Larsen (1969).

It is indeed fortunate that we have fungi to return the wood to a form that can be utilized by other plants and that we have insects that help also in this degradation process. It is, however, distressful to the wood-carver to experience an invasion of fungi or insects in his prized flitches, or worse yet, in his carvings. Care in the procurement of wood should be practiced at every turn to avoid these problems.

It was previously mentioned that cutting and felling of trees should be carried out at a time when adult insect movement and breeding are at a minimum. Cutting practices should be avoided in the spring when most insects emerge for reproduction and egg laying.

Functionally there are three types of insects: those that infest the areas just under the bark, those that work on the sapwood, and those that invade heartwood of even the hardest of our hardwoods (Findlay, 1967). If wood is cut in the spring and has been lying on the ground for a long period, one is sure to find larvae under the bark. Weakened trees are frequently exposed to the attacks of bark

FIGURE 48. Burrowing of bark beetles in cambium just below the bark. Note larvae as white grubs.

FIGURE 49. Powder-post beetle emergent holes in the sapwood of an old beam from a barn.

FIGURE 50. Frass from active borers at the base and near the top of an osage orange log.

beetles and the larvae of these can be found immediately under the bark. The trees generally present a sick or weakened condition when these destroyers of the cambium are in sufficient number (figure 48). A second group represented by the powder-post beetles can be found to occupy freshly cut wood or dried wood containing a band of sapwood. The powder-post beetle utilizes food within the sapwood as larvae and emerge from their perfectly cut round holes. Upon emergence, they go forth in reproduction and reinfestation (figure 49.) Borers, a third type of wood insect, are the largest of wood destroyers. The larvae may range from a quarter inch to almost two inches in length depending upon the species. These are very efficient wood destroyers. They leave a large tunnel of packed frass behind them (figure 50) and once this material is cleared

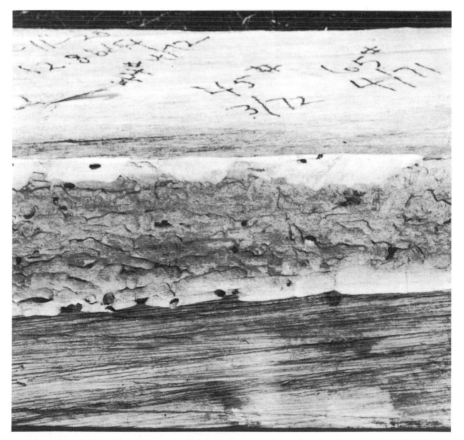

FIGURE 51. Tunnels of wood borers just under the bark of a black cherry prior to their burrowing into the sapwood and heartwood.

away their channels can be readily seen prior to their entering the deeper heartwood (figure 51).

High-temperature treatment in the home is again of no value. Spraying may kill the adults only after emergence; it cannot be expected that any kind of spraying will penetrate the innermost areas of the flitch where larvae are doing their damage. One may

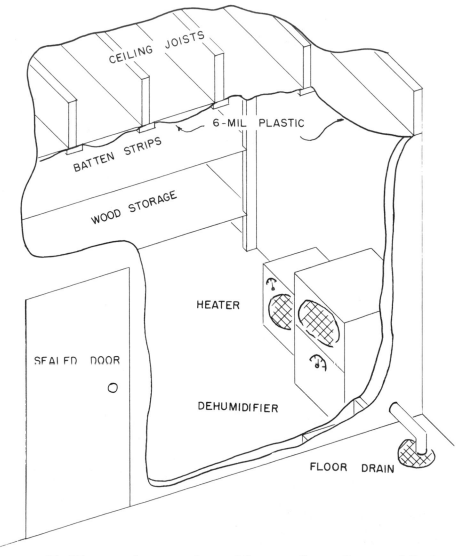

FIGURE 52. Diagram of construction and features of a small storage kiln for wood in the home.

upon working a particular flitch use an eyedropper or syringe of carbon tetrachloride at the entrance to any burrow. The flitch should be turned with the burrow end up, since carbon tetrachloride is heavier than air.

A last word of caution, avoid wherever possible any indication of infested wood. Examine carefully any flitch with bark intact that you are bringing to storage.

I have heard many wood-carvers and woodcraftsmen complain that they wish they could afford a dry kiln. Applying the principles of wood drying, that is, reduced humidity and higher heat, one can develop very simply a small kiln in a small part of a covered shed, the basement, or garage. Two-by-fours can be erected as studding to enclose a small area. This area can be lined with 6-mil plastic fitted with a gasket-sealed door and supplied with a small thermostatically controlled electric heater and dehumidifier. Although it is obvious from examination of figure 40 that humidity is the major environmental condition that brings about change in the moisture content of wood, heating of the storage area, especially in winter, is a constraint for the operation of the dehumidifier. Moisture cannot be extracted with a dehumidifier at temperatures near the freezing point. The dehumidifier is inoperative at low temperatures. The constraints of this system therefore require some heating. It should be minimal, however, to avoid too high a moisture differential from wood to surrounding air. Temperature and levels of relative humidity for operation can be selected from figure 40.

9

Carving the Flitch

After the long process of selecting wood, cutting and preparing it for drying, and waiting for months and maintaining records of the loss in weight, comes the pinnacle of the wood-carver's syndrome, that moment or period of anticipation when form begins to develop from the sculptor's eye to the sculptor's hand. Frequently seen is the statement that the sculptor or wood-carver positioned the form or determined where the form should lie within the flitch to maximize the figure of wood. This must be privy information or at least it would appear so since books on wood carving do not reveal the principles involved.

Where and how the sculptured form should fit within the flitch is a critical decision. George Nakashima, the woodcraftsman and artist of New Hope, Pennsylvania, states, "The hours spent by the true craftsman in bringing out the grain which has long been imprisoned in the trunk of the tree is an act of creation in itself" (Peet, 1957). When the wood-carver's eye first positions a figure in the concentric cylinders or section of a log, artistry begins. The simple annual rings exposed at the myriad planes of a carved surface create the figure every wood-carver looks forward to with keen anticipation. Mrs. Schuldenfrei in writing the poem dedicated to one of my birds felt and described this in a way most satisfactory to the wood-carver or sculptor (frontispiece).

Grain and figure are terms often confused; therefore, some clarification should be made at the outset. Grain refers to the cellular tissues of the tree. It has to do with the direction of wood fibers with respect to the axis of the trunk or limb. The more varied the cellular structure, the greater the potential for diversity of figure. The cell structure may vary by color, shape, thickness, and texture. Color may vary within the species through different influences of soil types and fertility of the location. In some woods, concentric yet irregular bands of color are laid down without reference to the annual rings. This is particularly apparent in Brazilian rosewood. The shape of cells vary among species, and these can be used to identify wood samples from various cuts of wood. A dry or moist condition creates differences in density of wood and stresses; knots and other abnormalities also add to differences in thicknesses within the cell structure. Early and late wood also add to contrast in figure. Texture, which has to do with the size and arrangement of cells, may be even or uneven. In even texture the cells, although nearly uniform, may be of fine or small size such as can be found in maple, cherry, and pine. Coarse cells can be found in the palms. Uneven texture, a mixture of fine and course cellular elements, can be noted in the ring-porous woods of oak and elm. Grain direction of wood fibers may be either simple or complex. Simple grain is straight and is characterized by the spruces and many pines. Complex grain structure produces the woods as described with the terms curly, wavey, spiral, ribbon, birdseye, etc. The expression of figure is further determined by the angle at which cuts are made to the concentric rings of growth. The wood-carver who can see the potential beauty of figure in a rough flitch is similar to the artist with camera who is able to translate what the eye sees to what the camera can image on the photoplate. These artistic abilities come from practice and constant awareness of the translation from rough to finished figures. A summary of factors that contribute to figure is given in table 11.

TABLE 11

FACTORS THAT INTERPLAY IN THE COMPLEXITY AND
DIVERSITY OF FIGURE IN WOOD

Variables of cellular structure:
    Color   ⎱ Species, color genetics, soil types
    Shape   ⎰ and soil fertility, weather, stresses
    Size   ⎱ (reaction wood) within wood and
    Density ⎰ location within the tree from which
               wood was cut.

Texture: size and arrangement of cells.
    Even
        Fine: cells small (maple and cherry)
        Course: (palm)
    Uneven
        Fine and course (oak and elm)

Grain: direction of wood fibers
    Simple: straight, unusual parallel to surface or cut
    Complex: curly, wavey, spiral, ribbon, fiddle back, birdseye, etc.

Angle of cut and fineness of finish

Sculptures made from an entire log are often seen at art shows or displays of wood carving. If the log is large, heart checks develop radially along the ray parenchyma, and splitting and cracking ensue. Wood-carvers without any knowledge of wood technology describe this as the "truth of the material." Why do they choose logs for carving? Is it because this is a convenient form from which to start? No, the log is a symmetrical form of concentric cylinders and the acute angles of the carved surface with the annual rings maximizes the development of figure. This is certainly well demonstrated in Douglas fir plywood or any other plywood where the cuts are made most closely to the concentric cylinders of wood.

If one cannot use a log because of the high potential of cracking, then how can one obtain maximum figure in using flitches as cut and described in the previous sections? Most carvings made from a radial flitch (figure 53) develop a simple figure because of the obtuse angle that occurs between the annual rings and the surface of the sculpture. A symmetrical sculpture with symmentrical figure can be developed with small dimension flitches that permit formation of acute angles with the surface of the sculpture (figure 53). If the sculptor wishes to maximize the complexity of structure, he may choose to position the form in such a manner in the flitch as to present both acute and obtuse angles of annual rings with the surface carving (figure 53). The carving of figure 7 from ring-porous Kentucky coffee tree exemplifies this type of positioning.

If one chooses to use a large billet similar to that shown with the annual ring formation in the middle figure 53, a decision must be made as to which face is the most important. The torso in black walnut (figure 54) was carved with the front of the body facing the pith of the tree. The broad expanse of the back faced the sapwood region of the flitch. Since this carving would take the shape of the solid line outline (figure 53), the length of the longer annual rings on the pith side are reduced. The torso is not presented as a broad flat piece on the pith side. The torso is rounded in front; therefore, tension is reduced and splitting is prevented on the pith side of the flitch. The broad expanse of the back, however, suffers the tendency to crack because of its exposure of an unbroken series of long annual rings. Summation of the shrinkage may be expressed with cracks developing in the outer part of the flitch.

A more complex figure could be developed if the front of the torso faced the sapwood region of the flitch (the dotted line positioning of figure 53). With this type of positioning, the figure is maximized. However, the potential for cracks occurring on the

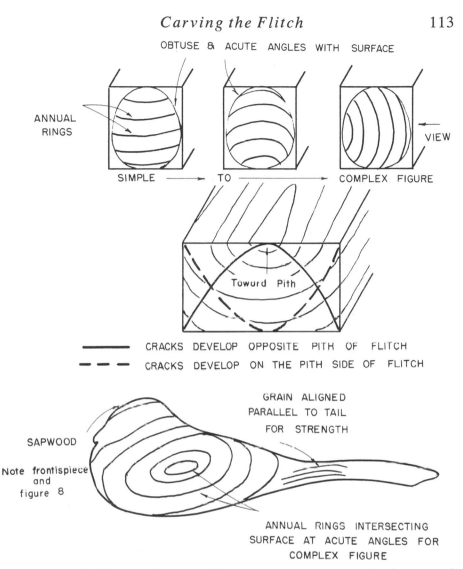

OBTUSE & ACUTE ANGLES WITH SURFACE

ANNUAL RINGS

VIEW

SIMPLE ⟶ TO ⟶ COMPLEX FIGURE

Toward Pith

──────── CRACKS DEVELOP OPPOSITE PITH OF FLITCH
── ── ── CRACKS DEVELOP ON THE PITH SIDE OF FLITCH

GRAIN ALIGNED PARALLEL TO TAIL FOR STRENGTH

SAPWOOD

Note frontispiece and figure 8

ANNUAL RINGS INTERSECTING SURFACE AT ACUTE ANGLES FOR COMPLEX FIGURE

FIGURE 53. Positioning figure in flitch for maximum strength, figure, and minimized cracking.

pith side of the billet are increased because of the differential in length of annular rings front and back.

Most wood-carvers learn one of the very common principles of positioning the figure as a means of obtaining strength in thin or weak structures. Horses are carved with the grain running vertically through the legs of the carving. This type of positioning has been practiced by the author in the development of all birds with long tails (frontispiece figure). The positioning in this carving gives

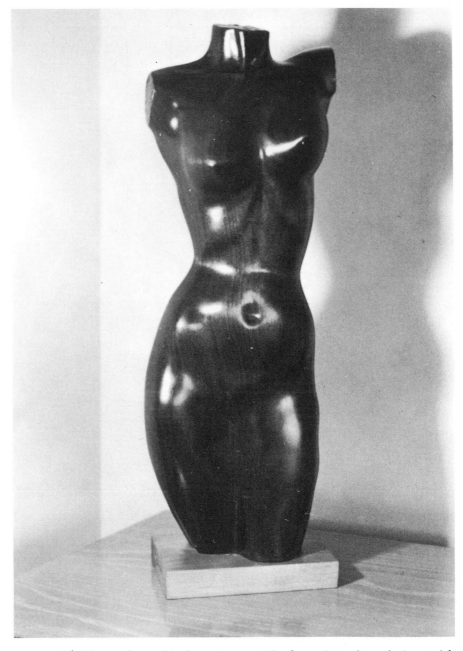

FIGURE 54. Torso from black walnut with frontal surface facing pith. Carved by author from billet measuring 6″ x 8″ x 24″.

strength to the tail where cellular structures are aligned parallel to the tail structure (figure 53). In like manner the birds of the frontispiece and figure 8 were positioned so as to utilize the sapwood of black walnut in the formation of a cap on the head of each bird. This latter type of modification type can be employed in the development of many other features needing emphasis.

Although this book was written primarily for those wishing to cut flitches of a single piece, lamination serves a distinct need when flitches of a given size cannot be obtained. There are times also when lamination meets a special need. This approach has merit and disadvantages. The craftsman or carver should recognize his demands and examine the possibilities of lamination (table 12).

TABLE 12

ADVANTAGES AND DISADVANTAGES OF LAMINATED FLITCHES

ADVANTAGES	DISADVANTAGES
1. Wood can be adequately dried before carving.	1. Contrasts of wood grain require care in cutting at the joint.
2. Much less chance of splitting.	2. Although all lamination should be done from the same board to reduce color change within the piece, any abrupt change in grain at joints often causes some color change simply because of the manner light strikes the grain.
3. Imperfections (knots, etc.) are avoided.	3. Figure is not continuous.
4. Larger pieces can be carved with more confidence of not cracking.	
5. Control of contrast can be obtained with lamination of species with different colors.	
6. Preferable if the carving is to be painted.	

There is an impropriety practiced among wood-carvers that should be eliminated. Sometimes a crack in a prized wood carving develops during an extremely cold period when atmospheric conditions of the home simulate those of the desert. Instructions of all types are given in various wood-carving books to fill the crack with wood matching the wood of the carving or a wedge of material, wax, or mixed sawdust and glue, etc. *Don't do this*. It should be recalled that wood equilibrates with atmospheric humidity and temperature. This was described in a previous section under equilibrium moisture content. Cracks developed under these extremely dry conditions will close during the more humid conditions of the following summer. Should the crack be filled during the dry winter period, the carving in adjusting to the more humid conditions will attempt to close over the filled material. Stresses developed under these conditions deepen the crack. Once such a fissure is developed, continued filling of the crack each winter will eventually split the carving. It is best to live with this circumstance and let the block or carvng adjust during the seasonal changes. I prefer, however, to place those large carvings in tight plastic bags during the winter. A small sponge with only a little water may be included.

Sometimes such a crack has developed because the flitch was not

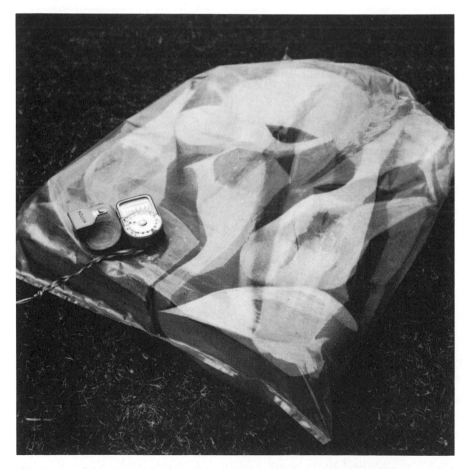

FIGURE 55. Pieces roughed out on bandsaw prior to their reaching equilibrium moisture constant. The plastic bag permits a slower loss of water and reduces checking.

adequately dried, or the flitch from which it was cut was unusually large. If a carving is to be cut from a small flitch, I frequently begin carving prior to the flitch having reached the equilibrium moisture content. Such carvings may be roughed out on the band saw and placed in a heavy plastic bag (figure 55). Between active periods of carving, the piece is kept tightly sealed in the plastic bag. Under these circumstances, tensions equilibrate within the flitch between the carving sessions. Upon nearing completion the carving may be removed alternate days to permit a gentle drying rate and redistribution of stresses set up during the short drying periods. If the atmospheric rate of change of humidity exceeds the capacity of the wood to equilibrate its internal humidity, stresses may develop that will lead to checking. I make a practice of keeping *all* my carvings in plastic bags between sessions of work. Thus, I further reduce the probability of checking.

CONCLUSION

I have attempted in the course of this book to pass on to you my experience and knowledge. I have tried not to introduce the wrong things for the right reasons or the right things for the wrong reasons. I have upon several occasions offered explanations that may have more basis in practice than in principle. You and I should continue to examine all ideas from an applied as well as theoretical point of view. Experimentation with adequate records still remain the order of the day. Hopefully you and I will follow Epictetus. I will continue to learn more about wood and thus fulfill a greater joy in its utilization. Will you travel with me down this delightful trail of the wood-carver-craftsman syndrome?

References

American Forest Association. 1971. American Forest Associations social register of big trees. *American Forest,* January, 1971: 25-31.

Anonymous. 1970. Nakashima the craftsman. (photographed by John Loengard) *Life* 68(22): 74-78.

Brough, J. C. S. 1969. *Timbers for Woodwork.* New York: Drake Publishers Ltd., 232 pp.

Brown, H. P., A. J. Panshin and C. C. Forsaith, 1952. Textbook of Wood Technology. Volume II, *The Physical, Mechanical and Chemical Properties of the Commercial Wood of the United States.* New York: McGraw-Hill Book Co., Inc., 783 pp.

Carstenson, Cecil C. (Edited by William S. Brown). 1971. *The Craft and Creation of Wood Sculpture.* New York: Charles Scribner's Sons, 179 pp.

Fergus, Charles L. 1960. *Illustrated Genera of Wood Decay Fungi.* Minneapolis: Burgess Publishing Co., 132 pp.

Findlay, W. P. K. 1967. *Timber Pests and Disease.* New York: Pergamon Press, 280 pp.

Harlow, William M. 1970. *Inside Wood, Masterpiece of Nature.* Washington, D.C.: Amer. Forestry Assoc., 120 pp.

Harrar, E. S. 1957. *Hough's Encyclopedia of American Woods.* New York: Robert Speller and Sons. Fifteen volumes with wood specimens included.

Hutchins, Carleen Maley. 1962. The physics of violins. *Scientific American* 214(11): 14 pp.

———. 1967. Founding a family of fiddles. *Physics Today* 20(2): 23-37.

Joyce, M. Ernest. 1970. *Encyclopedia of Furniture Making.* London: Drake Publications Limited, 494 pp.

Koehler, Arthur. 1924. *The Properties and Uses of Wood.* New York: McGraw-Hill Book Co., 354 pp.

Kozlowski, T. T. 1971. *Growth and Development of Trees,* vol. I. New York: Academic Press, 443 pp.

McMinn, Howard E. and Evelyn Maino. 1951. *An Illustrated Manual of Pacific Coast Trees.* Berkeley, California: Univ. of Calif. Press, 409 pp.

Panshin, A. J. and Carl de Zeeuw. 1970. *Textbook of Wood Technology* (third edition). New York: McGraw-Hill Book Co., 705 pp.

Peet, Creighton. 1957. Quality. *American Forests* 63(6): 12-5; 65-66.

Petrides, George A. 1972. *A Field Guide to Trees and Shrubs.* Boston: Houghton Mifflin Co., 428 pp.

Preston, Richard J., Jr. 1968. *Rocky Mountain Trees.* New York: Dover Publications Inc., 285 pp.

Rich, Jack C. 1970. *Sculpture in Wood.* New York: Oxford University Press, 155 pp.

Rietz, Raymond C. and Rufus H. Page. 1971. Air drying of lumber: A guide to industry practice. *U. S. Forest Service Agric. Handbook* 402: 110 pp.

Shigo, Alex L. and Edwin H. Larson. 1969. *A photo guide to the patterns of discoloration and decay in living northern hardwood trees.* U.S.D.A. Forest Service Research Paper N.E. 127: 100 pp.

United States Department of Agriculture. 1941. *Climate and Man,* 1941 *Yearbook of Agriculture, Supt. Documents,* Washington, D.C., 1248 pp.

————. 1949. *Trees,* 1949 Yearbook of Agriculture, Supt. of Documents, Washington, D.C.

Werner, Erteld, H. J. Mette and W. Achterberg. 1964. *Defects in Wood.* London: Leonard Hill Ltd., 76 pp., 188 figures.

Index